Essays Eucharistic Sacrifice in the Early Church:

A Sequel to Liturgical Study No. 31
Eucharistic Sacrifice: The Roots of a Metaphor, **By Rowan Williams**

Edited by
Colin Buchanan

CONTENTS AND CONTRIBUTORS

	Page
1. **Eucharist, Sacrifice, and Scripture** by Michael Vasey (Lecturer at Cranmer Hall, Durham).....................................	3
2. **'A Semantic Voyage'** by David Gregg (Principal, Romsey House, Cambridge)	10
3. **Christ's Priesthood and 'Eucharistic Sacrifice'—an 'Historical' Axe to a 'Metaphorical' Root?** by Christopher Hancock (Assistant Curate, Holy Trinity Church, Leicester)......................	15
4. **'Doing Theology in Heaven'** by Nicholas Sagovsky (Vice-Principal, Coates Hall, Episcopal Theological College, Edinburgh)........	22
5. **Eucharistic Sacrifice—What can We Learn from Christian Antiquity?** by Kenneth Stevenson (Anglican Chaplain and Lecturer in Liturgy, University of Manchester)	26
6. **A Response** by Rowan Williams (Lecturer in Divinity, University of Cambridge)	33

GROVE BOOKS
BRAMCOTE   NOTTS.   NG9 3DS

EDITORIAL INTRODUCTION

I have myself been engaged in controversy about eucharistic sacrifice—sometimes even in hand-to-hand fighting—for upwards of twenty years, during which time I have dissented on the Liturgical Commission over the oblation of the bread and cup, joined with two anglo-catholics in writing agreed theology in *Growing Into Union* (1970), shadowed the Anglican-Roman Catholic Agreement on the Eucharist (1971), and published in many ways on the subject. After some preliminary shots, there came opportunity in this series to publish R. P. C. Hanson's *Eucharistic Offering in the Early Church* (Liturgical Study no. 19, 1979). This seemed to throw down a demanding intellectual gauntlet to current anglo-catholic verbalization of beliefs and liturgical desiderata on eucharistic sacrifice, and the Group for Renewal of Worship went hunting for a representative anglo-catholic to respond to the Hanson material. In time, Rowan Williams (whilst not necessarily accepting the 'representative' role) agreed to write, and he came and addressed a meeting of the Group and was duly commissioned. His Study, beautifully (if even more demandingly) executed, was no. 31 *Eucharistic Sacrifice: The Roots of a Metaphor* (1982). No-one viewed the matter as completed at that point, and the Group held a conference with Rowan Williams, and with Kenneth Stevenson invited as an extra guest, from which this Symposium has come.

Part of the problem hitherto has been, as Kenneth Stevenson notes, a failure to come to close encounter over the issues. In part evangelicals have been left wondering whether anglo-catholics would not take up *any* ground so long as it allowed them to say that the eucharist is in some sense a 'sacrifice'. Certainly there is a linguistic basis for this in the second century and thereafter, and a significance for it will be argued by Rowan Williams. But the exposition does alter with succeeding generations. What, one might well know wonder, has happened to that erstwhile 'key' concept 'anamnesis'? Once it was the great biblical and patristic foundation which (with all sorts of Jewish background) established the 'making present of an event of the past'. Now it has vanished from sight. Rowan Williams has taken different ground, but has stoutly defended the concept of the eucharist as Christian sacrifice. The purpose of this Syposium is to see whether he could or should be prised from that ground, or at least whether the quotation below from Bishop Stephen Neill can be in some part transcended.

Perhaps a liturgist might also ask that discussion should not get detached from what we are to say and do at the eucharist—some expositions seem simply to forget the bread and wine and their liturgical context. It seems reasonable to ask that any defence of, e.g. 'we offer to you this bread and this cup' should not only discuss our relationship with Christ's eternal priesthood, but should also demonstrate how this is expressed distinctively in the liturgical celebration in such a way as to lead us to conclude that 'do this in remembrance of me' *entails* 'therefore, Father, in remembrance of him we offer...'.

Colin Buchanan

THE STEPHEN NEILL QUOTATION

(originally cited by Christopher Hancock, but omitted through lack of space in his chapter, which it would have closed, and referred to by Rowan Williams on page 37).

'It is impossible to pretend that those two views, even stated moderately, are ultimately reconcilable, as different emphases within a common understanding. They do depend on very deep differences in belief as to the nature of God and his action in the world. There is therefore a real tension in the Anglican communion, and nothing is to be gained by avoiding it or pretending it does not exist'. (S. C. Neill, 'The Holy Communion in the Anglican Church', in H. Martin (ed.) *The Holy Communion* (London, 1947), pp.65-6).

THE COVER PICTURE

is of the mosaic of the Empress Theodora with her court at Ravenna

Copyright Grove Books and the respective authors 1984

First Impressions December 1984

ISSN 0306–0608
ISBN 0 907536 82 4

1. EUCHARIST, SACRIFICE AND SCRIPTURE
by Michael Vasey

What's in a word?
'I have regarded it as fitting . . . to declare what I have learned from the Holy Scriptures, making a sparing use of titles and words which are not found literally in Holy Writ, even though they preserve the sense of the Scriptures.' writes Basil the Great in his *Morals*.[1] Christians have often felt it right to go beyond the terminology of scripture, but have commonly felt a certain embarassment in so doing, at least when challenged. Athanasius and other defenders of *homoousios* ('of the same substance') had to answer objections that this banner of Nicene orthodoxy was not scriptural.[2]

Often a scriptural word, even one that occurs rarely, has become the focus—or indeed the title—of a doctrine. One verse, John 1.14, has given Christian doctrine and worship the term 'Incarnation'. Such development can be seen within scripture itself—for example the word 'image'.[3] What may seem a fruitful development for many centuries can find itself being by-passed as a new generation in the church feels it does less than justice to the general sense of scripture. Two modern examples are 'sanctification' as a technical term in the theology of the Christian life, and 'priest' as a title for an ordained minister.

An instructive example is the use of the term 'bishop' for the chief pastor of an area. Hooker acknowledges that this usage is narrower than that in the New Testament, but defends the development as entirely proper. He argues that the office existed before the name; 'generally things are ancienter than the names whereby they are called.'[4] Modern Anglican evangelicals defend this particular extension of scriptural use on the grounds of the symbolic appropriateness of the office of bishop as we have received it from the ancient church.[5] Although this use of the term is not required by the New Testament and indeed may even seem at odds with the scriptural use, it is 'commended by necessity of fitness'. The institution and its name are defended on the grounds that it clearly and helpfully witnesses to central gospel truths. There is, of course, the danger (which *Growing into Union* avoids) that the potency of its symbolism may lead some to say 'apart from episcopacy there can be no Church'.

Why have Christians felt themselves reluctant to go beyond the terminology of scripture in controversial areas? The first reason is a desire to do justice to the unique authority of Apostolic teaching preserved for us in the New Testament. ARCIC speaks of it as

---
[1] *Ascetical Works* (The Catholic University of America Press, 1950) p.58.
[2] *Defence of the Nicene Definition* 21, cf. J. N. D. Kelly *Early Christian Doctrines* (3rd edition, A. C. Black, 1965) p.46.
[3] TEV seems to ignore this way words function, cf. Gen. 1.27.
[4] *Ecclesiastical Polity*, Book VII ch. ii.2.
[5] e.g. Colin Buchanan, E. L Mascall, J. I. Packer, The Bishop of Willesden *Growing into Union* (SPCK, 1970) pp.68, 75-77.

'normative'.[1] Austin Farrer calls it 'decisive'.[2] He points out that it is not enough to view the apostles as important human witnesses of the revelation of Christ. 'The interpretative work of the Apostles must be understood as participation in the mind of Christ, thorugh the Holy Ghost. . . . the express thought of Christ is extended in the Apostolic teaching.'[1] A second reason is the fact that scripture is the common possession of the whole church. The reading of the Bible in public and private is always a major influence on the way Christians think. Dissonance between the scriptural use of a word and a more specialized or developed use is quickly felt. (Note the way modern translations of the Bible do not translate *episcopos* as 'bishop'.)

How do we judge whether a particular development of a term beyond the scriptural use is appropriate? A number of criteria suggest themselves. Does it do justice to the sense of scripture? Is the dissonance with scriptural use tolerable? Is its use helpful or necessary for grasping some truth in worship or doctrine? Can it be used confidently and creatively? Does its use divide the church? Does its use aid fellowship with the wider church across the world or across the centuries?

A short paper cannot go far in exploring how these criteria apply to the description of the eucharist as a sacrifice. The answers people give to the last two questions are, I think, shaped by which parts of the church they know or love. The rest of the paper is addressed to the first four.

Sacrifice today

The term 'sacrifice' is used in many different, even contradictory, ways today. Strictly it is a ritual term referring to the killing of an animal or person or the surrender of an object, generally in a religious context. However the popular Western use today is the giving up of something for the sake of something else with no thought of a God dimension. This widespread 'secular' use probably means that many modern Christians mishear the word and understand it primarily as referring to costly giving up. At the same time it is the religious and cultic association of terms like 'sacrifice' and 'priest' (applied to all Christians) that makes them attractive today. With so many cultural assumptions that exclude God or define human beings in scientific or economic terms we sense liberation in cultic language as many charismatic choruses demonstrate. Rowan Williams has this exactly right when he says 'the effect of Christ's sacrifice is precisely to make us "liturgical" beings, capable of offering ourselves, our praises and our symbolic gifts to a God who we know will receive us in Christ.'[4] Again 'We are always in danger of *regression* in Christian life: the basic fact of our unqualified dependence on grace can become an alibi, a refusal to assume the

---

[1] *Final Report* (S.P.C.K., 1982) p.52.
[2] *The Glass of Vision* (Dacre Press, 1948) p.42.
[3] *ibid.* p.42. Note also, 'The New Testament books may not be at the centre of the process of Pentecostal inspiration, but they are our only direct clue to its nature.' (p.55).
[4] Rowan Williams *Eucharistic Sacrifice—the Roots of a Metaphor* (Grove Liturgical Study no. 31, 1982) p.27. I return to 'our symbolic gifts' on p.9 below.

EUCHARIST, SACRIFICE AND SCRIPTURE

authority we have as baptized Christians . . . We have been given our selves, our Christian selves, as a free gift: to trust God means also to trust ourselves and our worth in his eyes.'

The irony is that sacrificial language does not always lead to a Christian notion of self-worth. Suzanne Campbell-Jones in anthropological study of two congregations of working nuns found a profound difference in their understanding of personal sacrifice. One community saw sacrifice as sharing in death through self-abnegation; the other understood it as developing and consecrating the talents of the nuns.[1] In secular and evangelical circles the term also works in either direction. How the notion of sacrifice operates depends on what value is given to the human person as he or she relates to God. It is often assumed that emphasis on propitiatory sacrifice is necessarily linked with the view that God is hostile to us as persons.[2] This seems to me false as a matter of history, and to rest on a confusion—on a failure to observe that it is the implicit understanding of the human person which determines how any notion of sacrifice is received. For much Roman Catholic and evangelical Christianity ideas of propitiatory sacrifice work to affirm the value of the human person. It is a sign of the good purpose God has for us, of the seriousness with which he treats us, that our sin provokes his just displeasure; it is because he loves us that he stands with us and bears our sin for us.[3]

Also today, awareness of tribal cultures and their formal analysis in the discipline of anthropology are giving us a more positive view of animal sacrifice than used to prevail in the Western world. Protests about animal suffering look hypocritical in the face of the remote but widespread cruelty of modern farming methods. Sacrifices are seen to be part of complex ritual systems that bring into the public arena realities of value, social order, conflict, sin and responsibility which our more sophisticated society can only handle through money, our primary symbol of value, and which we frequently refuse to acknowledge by shutting people away in institutions. At the same time sacrifice is not simply a social mechanism—it relates our tangible existence to the 'world of non-material powers and forces assumed and believed . . . to exist'.[4]

Sacrifice is a sort of physical prayer and this means that there are no general answers to questions about the meaning of sacrifice, or even to what constitutes a sacrifice. Just as there are many different motives

---

[1] *Sacrifice* eds. M. F. C. Bourdillon and M. Fortes (London and New York 1980) p.103.

[2] I sense that this assumption is present in *Eucharistic Sacrifice—the Roots of a Metaphor*, and in Frances Young, *The Use of Sacrificial Ideas in Greek Christian Writers from the New Testament to John Chrysostom* (Cambridge, Mass. 1979) and *Sacrifice and the Death of Christ* (S.P.C.K., 1975).

[3] From where, then, does this low view of the human person come which corrupts so much Christian life? I think the answer includes: the natural self-hatred of the sinner, a weak doctrine of creation in a church which underplays the Old Testament, and the tendency of the church to despise the secular. It is significant that Rowan Williams' best examples of sacrificial imagery come from a semitic milieu.

[4] M. Fortes in *Sacrifice* p.ix.

for prayer, and many different assumptions about God underlying prayer, so the same is true for sacrifice. It is always relevant to ask both what this individual means by his sacrifice, and what this society means by the sacrifice. Anthropologists warn against generalizations or extrapolations about sacrifice from one context to another.

Sacrifice in Scripture

Even a brief glance at any modern account of Old Testament sacrifice shows that we are dealing not with a simple rite but with an interlocking and developing system.[1] There is not one main term for sacrifice but at least eight. There are at least five types of sacrifice and these are undergirded by intricate rules of procedure. This complex system interlocks with the complex symbolic systems of ritual purity and with that of the layout, furniture, and personnel, of the temple. One way of understanding this whole system is to see it as a complex dramatic language that uses significant symbols and ideas of Israel's life.[2] The intricate pattern then corresponds to the grammar of the language. In order to understand the meaning of part of the system we need to begin to perceive the values and life of the whole community[3], and to see them in their context of the story of God's deliverance and his covenant.[4]

The analogy of a language is also useful because, like a language, the sacrificial system evolved and adapted with time and changing social structures.[5] This may give a certain plausibility to Rowan Williams' statement, 'part of the assumption of this study is that, in Old and New Testament alike, the concept of sacrifice is a fluid one'.[6] However this begs the question of whether there are there any fixed strands in the evolving grammar of biblical sacrifice. The fact of the diaspora and, for Christians, the opening of the kingdom to the Gentiles led to the collapse of much of the grammar. Certain theological constants remain: God's steadfast love and his righteousness. (It is interesting that the attempted resolution of these in the fourth servant song draws on sacrificial language, portraying the Lord's servant as both scapegoat and sin offering).

Equally enduring seems to be the notion that the basic counter of the sacrificial system is an unblemished domestic animal offered and killed with its blood poured out. The animals's blood, expressive of its life poured out in death,[7] is God's gracious gift 'to make atonement'.[8] There is an important duality here: the animal is simultaneously God's

---

[1] e.g. art. 'Sacrifice and Offerings, OT' by J. Milgrom in *Interpreter's Dictionary of the Bible* Supplementary Volume 1976. Also J. W. Rogerson in *Sacrifice* pp.44ff.

[2] e.g. Douglas Davies, *Zeitschrift fur die Alttestamentliche Wissenschaft* (1977) p.387. Mary Douglas *Purity and Danger*.

[3] This is helpfully summarized and illustrated in G. J. Wenham *Numbers* (IVP, 1981) pp.25-39. See also pp.202-205 and his *Levicitus* (Hodder, 1979).

[4] J. W. Rogerson in *Sacrifice* pp.56-58.

[5] Not to mention tension between popular *versus* official religion—see J. W. Rogerson *ibid.* p.46.

[6] *ibid.* p.26.

[7] See chapter 3 of Leon Morris *The Apostolic Preaching of the Cross* (Tyndale, 1965).

[8] The same term is used in non-cultic settings to mean 'to pay a ransom'—a common and humane feature of Ancient Near Eastern Law. See G. J. Wenham *Leviticus* pp.57-62 and at Lev. 17.11.

gracious provision of a ransom, and man's willing offering of himself. Both sides of this duality are present in the New Testament. Paul twice picks up the lovely Old Testament phrase of a fragrant or sweet-smelling sacrifice to say that our obedience and love are pleasant to God, although in its original context the idea of atonement is also present.[1]

What happens in the New Testament, it seems, is that sacrifice seen as God's gracious provision of atonement is referred only to the death of Christ, while the other aspect of sacrifice is applied both to Christ and to Christians. Jesus' death was not, of course, a cultic act; it is spoken of as a sacrifice precisely to emphasize its religious meaning.[2] It is because the death of Christ draws to itself all that sacrificial imagery has to say about atonement that the same language is available in the New Testament without such overtone to give a Godward dimension to Christian obedience (Rom. 12.1), worship (Heb. 13.15), alms (Heb. 13.16), martyrdom (Phil. 2.17), even cash for a link missionary (Phil. 4.18).

Eucharist and Sacrifice

Two facts are clear: the New Testament never speaks of the eucharist as a sacrifice, and the early church very quickly began to do so. The reason for the former seems to be the very close association between the new ritual and the death of Christ. So sharp is the sense that the death of Christ has drawn to itself all that sacrificial language says about atonement, that it is unthinkable in the New Testament to speak of the eucharist as a sacrifice. To partake of the eucharist is to partake of the sacrifice of Christ (1 Cor. 10.16); therefore the eucharist is not a sacrifice.

Why then did the early church so quickly adopt the term for the eucharist? Rowan Williams sets out very clearly the process. Christians needed to rebut the charge that they were irreligious, and without religious rites. The popular term for a cultic act was 'sacrifice' and so Christians applied the term to the eucharist. They did not imply that it was 'offered for sins' because sin had been dealt with in the death of Christ and because contemporary philosophy had no time for propitiatory sacrifice—rejecting as unworthy of the gods what was really a parody of the biblical view.[3]

Rowan Williams writes, 'There is no doubt for Justin that the eucharist is "structurally" a sacrifice'[4], and he quotes with approval Adrian

---

[1] Jerusalem Bible translates Lev. 1.17 etc. 'its fragrance will appease Yahweh'.
[2] Note Paul's introduction of sacrificial language into a forensic context in Rom. 3.21-26. It is the dimension of religious meaning that makes Stephen Sykes assert that sacrifice is used realistically and not metaphorically of the death of Christ (*Sacrifice* pp.62-63).
[3] 'The distinctiveness of the OT usage being its recognition first that God's wrath, unlike all human wrath, is perfectly righteousness, and therefore free from every trace of irrationality, caprice and vindictiveness, and secondly that in the process of averting this righteous wrath from man it is God himself who takes the initiative.' (C. E. B. Cranfield *Romans* (I.C.C., 1975) p.216).
[4] *ibid.* p.8.

Hastings' comment, 'The eucharist fulfils all the obvious criteria for sacrifice outlined by the anthropologist'.[1] This may be, but the eucharist is not a sacrifice within the simplified grammar of the biblical system.[2] Once the eucharist is called a sacrifice in any sense it begins to resonate with the biblical notion of sacrifice. The result is the shifting kaleidoscope of sacrificial imagery and theology that has marked much eucharistic theology since then. The way is open for obscuring 'the brilliance of a light so dazzling that it absorbs all other lights'.[3]

How successful are modern attempts to shake the kaleidoscope? ARCIC is sufficiently coy about speaking of the eucharist as sacrifice that one imagines an ARCIC liturgy would hardly use the term. Yet the new Missal prays,

V. Pray, brethren, that our sacrifice may be acceptable to God, the almighty Father.

R. May the Lord accept the sacrifice at your hands for the praise and glory of his name, for our good, and the good of all his church.

This goes against the way the New Testament resolves the duality of sacrificial imagery, and implies that our eucharist in some sense draws down God's favour.

Rite A's first two eucharistic prayers may be successful as a political compromise, but the language of sacrifice hardly engages the mind and imagination of the worshipper. The attempt to contain the resonance of a powerful word results in flat banality.[4] Gerald Bray is right to complain 'that the objective character of Christ's work on the cross as an atoning sacrifice has been supplanted . . . by a more subjective approach . . . it is assumed that "the benefits of Christ's passion" have already been received'.[5] We need, in my view, to abandon the effort to treat a powerful image as if we were lawyers with a hostile witness. Our liturgies should affirm strongly the atoning achievement of Christ's

---

[1] *ibid.* p.31. The reference in the footnote to A. Hayley's work is not relevant as the assumptions underlying Assamese Hinduism naturally differ from the biblical tradition.

[2] An example of what can happen if you ignore this can be seen in Bernard Cooke's *Sacrament and Sacramentality* (Twenty-Third Publications, 1983). He tries to cut through the complex system by saying 'none was more basic than the peace offering, which in its essentials was a covenant meal shared by Yahweh and his people.' (p.106). Sacrifice becomes loving self-gift (p.109): 'What did Jesus actually do in the action of his Passover, beginning with the supper and extending through through his death into his resurrection? Basically, he gave himself to his friends' (p.108).

[3] Lucien Deiss on Christ's priesthood and sacrifice in *It's the Lord's Supper* (Collins, 1976) p.87.

[4] David Power arguing that 'the ecumenical solution is not wholly satisfactory' writes of 'the rather banal explanation of the eucharist which carries us no further than the harmless observation that the Church now offers herself along with the offering of Christ' in Kevin Seasoltz (ed.) *Living Bread, Saving Cup* (The Liturgical Press, Collegeville, Minnesota, 1982)) p.158.

[5] *Sacrament and Ministry in Ecumenical Perspective* (Latimer Study 18, 1984) p.4.

sacrificial death, should plead that we may continue to receive its benefits, and should deploy cultic language to portray the life his death has made possible.

Attempts to define, despite scripture, a precise sense in which the eucharist may be called a sacrifice, prevent our liturgy focussing where it should. The following untidy suggestion of where we might go has Syrian anaphoras as its inspiration:

People: Your death, Lord, we commemorate, your resurrection we confess, and your second coming we await.

Priest: Remembering your death for our sins . . . we ask that you will give us life through your resurrection life, and purify us through your sacrificial and life-giving death, that we may stand in holiness and offer to you our prayers, our whole lives, and our service of others. As your royal priesthood we pray that you will have mercy on all men, that you will heal the world you have made, and that you will bestow on your people the gifts of your Holy Spirit . . .

What then of the bread and wine as 'our symbolic gifts'? I cannot do better then give three quotations from a fine essay by the Roman Catholic liturgist, David Power.

'Jesus' words (over the cup) recall the blood ritual of such sacrifices as the passover and the covenant. In these, the blood ritual has not the implications of offering but signifies God's mercy to man.'[1]

'Irenaeus does not pass from one offering to another, but positing a first offering then abandons the image and speaks instead of what God gives us in the body and blood.'[2]

'A literal offering of bread and wine has in the course of time been included in the eucharistic ritual. This is not essential to it, but when added draws out the symbolism of the Eucharist in certain directions. It relates the mystery of redemption to the mystery of creation, it associates the community with humanity's religious and secular strivings, and in the reminder of our own finitude which comes in this abortive gesture there is already a remembering of the grace which is given to us in the gift of the body and blood of Christ.'[3]

What liturgical text should appropriately accompany this 'abortive gesture'?

---

[1] *ibid.* p.163.
[2] *ibid.* p.167.
[3] *ibid.* p.174.

2. A SEMANTIC VOYAGE?
by David Gregg

Rowan Williams's allusion to the 'mist-shrouded lower levels' of this debate[1] calls to mind an experience well up on Scafell Pike. Encountering a Warden in thick mist we asked how far it was to the top. 'About 25,000 miles the way you're going!' we were told. It appeared that our last compass reading had been taken near a notorious crop of magnetic rock and had sent us significantly off course! Whilst greatly appreciating the eirenic spirit of Dr. Williams's monograph, and sharing fully his declared agenda of rehabilitating a sacramental approach and sacrificial language in eucharistic theology in an appropriate way, as my previous contribution to this debate was intended to demonstrate[2], it occurs to me that our attempts to reach 'the clarities of the visible summit' are perhaps being similarly vitiated by an unsuspected source of 'false readings'. Statements like

'We do not work our salvation in *offering the eucharistic oblation* . . . the purity of *our offering* depends upon our commitment to the Christ through whom *it is offered.*' (L.S. 31, p.11)

focus the issue admirably. Our prime concern will be with the use of the English words 'offer/offering', and the suspicion that *this* may be the offending lodestone. This paper is a further attempt to advance the discussion on a subtle and somewhat elusive point, in the hope that, in our mutual quest for an understanding of God's truth in this area, we may perhaps 'climb on' with more accurate bearings.

1. The Significance of the Issue

One has only to do a word-count in Dr. Williams's own monograph to discover the centrality of 'offer/offering' language in his examination of the 'propriety of sacrificial language' (L.S. 31, p.6). For those who resist the incursion of the theology of eucharistic sacrifice, such language has become a definitive shibboleth. So that, for instance,

'We *offer* you . . . this life-giving bread . . . this saving cup . . .'

or 'We *offer* you . . . this holy and living sacrifice'

or 'We *offer* you . . . his body and blood' (the formulae in the new Roman Catholic rites) are identified as the epitome of the 'Sacrifice of the Mass'; the chief bone of contention[3] in the published eucharist in the 'Proposals' of the Churches' Council for Covenanting was centred on '. . . we *offer* you these holy gifts and ourselves with them, one holy, living sacrifice'; and, no doubt, discussion of the Lima eucharist will similarly centre around the suspicion that, 'Behold, Lord, this eucharist which you yourself gave to the Church and graciously receive it, as you *accept the offering* [N.B. present tense!] of your Son . . .' is a barely concealed formula along the same lines.[4] Far from being a mere quibble, it would appear that some consideration of the semantics involved could help to identify a residual problem in this whole discussion.

---

[1] *Eucharistic Sacrifice—The Roots of a Metaphor* (Grove Liturgical Study no. 31) p.5.
[2] *Anamnesis in the Eucharist* (Grove Liturgical Study no. 5, 1976)—currently out of print.
[3] So, e.g., Prof. D. R. Jones, in his speech in the General Synod debate in July 1980]
[4] Especially when interpreted by the ealier rendering of Deut. 16.1?

2. Patristic Fundamentalism
For those who are completely diverted by the use of 'offer' language in the central eucharistic act, the methodology of Dr. Williams' Study alienates them almost before he starts. One can hardly accuse him of being a 'patristic fundamentalist' on the basis of a thirty-three page monograph, especially when (a) he had been *asked* to do a patristic study, and (b) his other recorded pronouncements on the subject are taken into consideration; but he cannot help but encourage those whose main argument is 'the Fathers had it right', when he appeals to the likes of Ignatius, Justin Martyr, Irenaeus, Ephrem etc. (and even Philo!) as his main authorities, with almost no direct examination of the *biblical* basis for his case. 'The propriety of sacrificial language' in this context, and especially the prolific use of the notion of 'offer/offering' in respect of the elements, has to be argued on more convincing grounds to satisfy those who suspect that *either* the 'Fathers' may not have attached the same nuances to their Greek and Latin 'offer/offering' vocabulary as their latter-day English-speaking interpreters suppose;[1] *or else,* if they did, they had their basic biblical theology wrong! Either way, some consideration of the antecedent biblical (and particularly Hebraic) evidence might throw light on the matter, and to this we now turn.

3. Hebraic Antecedents
. . . (a) Vocabulary of Sacrifice: There is no space here to develop the theme, but even a cursory exmination of the 'roots' of the Hebrew terminology of sacrifice reveals that 'offer/offering' language is, at very least, uncalled for. Other renderings are *always* intrinsically more accurate. The 'OLAH is, 'that-which-goes-up, (i.e. Burnt), the MINCHAH is 'present/tribute'; the ZEBACH is 'that-which-is-slaughtered'; the ASHAM is 'that-which-is-for-guilt' etc. Likewise the verbs, often in Hiphil forms. For many sacrifices a cognate form is found, so that the 'OLAH 'goes up', the ZEBACH is 'slaughtered', the MINCHAH is 'presented, given in tribute' etc. Others are basically 'brought close' (QRB) or 'brought near' (NGSH).[2]

Yet the English versions are almost unanimous in translating the nouns by burnt-, cereal-, peace-, guilt-OFFERING etc. and the verbs (almost indiscriminately) by OFFER.

. . . (b) A Particular Example: It may be instructive to trace a particular 'case in point' through its various stages of translation (Hebrew, Greek, Latin, English), and, since Dr. Williams' begins with the patristic appropriation of Mal. 1.11 (which the N.T. writers singularly failed to make directly!) perhaps *it* would serve the purpose. In the immediate context (vv.6-14) the RSV uses 'offer/offering' forms seven times, *viz.* for NGSH in verses 7, 8 (twice) and 11, and for

---
[1] In the case of Ephrem's Syriac, on Dr. Williams' own evidence, this is certainly the case. On p.21 he (twice) points out that it is the Semitic root *qrb* for which the 'offering' translations are offered (!) and on p.27 he rightly points out that this means *'brought close',* (before going on to suggest the (gratuitous?) alternative 'or *offered'!*)
[2] With QRB arguably emphasizing the 'approach', and NGSH, the 'arrival, touching'.

MINCHAH in verses 10, 11 and 13. The renderings in verse 11 can hardly, therefore, be regarded as arbitrary or casual. In verse 11 itself, where the Hebrew is: MUQTAR *MUGGASH* (✓ NAGASH) LISHMI *UMINCHAH* TeHORAH, the Septuagint has:
 thumiama *prosagetai* (✓ prosago) to onomati kai *thusia* kathara
and the Vulgate rendering is:
 Sacrificatur et *offertur* (✓ offero) nomini meo *oblatio* munda.

In the EVV, the RSV rendering:
 '. . . incense *is offered* to my name and a pure *offering*' follows the AV and RV (Margin—'incense and a pure *oblation* are *offered.*'), and is echoed by NASV and JB. NEB has '*are offered*' corresponding to MUGGASH, but 'gifts' for MINCHAH. GNB has 'they burn incense to me and *offer* acceptable sacrifices', and NIV, 'incense and pure *offerings* will be brought to my name'. It is the contention of this paper that somewhere along the way from NAGASH/MINCHAH to OFFER/OFFERING a significant semantic transmogrification has occurred. A (necessarily brief) lexical survey will hopefully give some indication where.

4. A Semantic Voyage?

We have suggested above the basic meanings of the Hebrew, and can find no lexical excuse *per se* for anything but the intrinsically pragmatic renderings for NAGASH (bring near) or MINCHAH (present/tribute) suggested. Likewise the Greek lexica (e.g. Liddell and Scott/Arndt and Gingrich etc.) give the obvious 'bring forward, bring to, conduct' etc. for *prosago* (with no hint of 'offer' nuances at least in the pre-patristic period) and the basic 'sacrifice' (from the root *thuo*=slaughter, kill) for *thusia*, though here the rendering 'offering' *does* sometimes appear, but without explanation! It is when we turn to the Latin lexica that the seeds of suspicion of a subtle transformation really begin to sprout. From a basic 'to bring before' (=ob-fero), to 'present, offer, show, exhibit' for *offero*, Lewis and Short give, *inter alia* the particular meaning 'to offer, *proffer*, to bring, cause, occasion, *confer, bestow . . .*'

Likewise, identifying *oblatio* as participle of the same verb, they give 'an offering, presenting, *a giving or bestowing gratuitously*', and a particular meaning of '*a bid at an auction*'. The Oxford Latin Dictionary reinforces this latter by including '*tender*' amongst its renderings for *oblatio,* and for *offero* has (again, *inter alia*):

1. To put in a person's 'path, cause to be encountered.

4. To present as something to be taken note of, bring to or force upon someone's attention.

8. To hold out (a material thing) for a person to take . . .

9a. To tender for acceptance, offer (help, resources).

I have deliberately left till now any direct semantic examination of the English, in the hope that, with this build-up, the reader may, like me, have sensed (uneasily?) that things are moving a bit off course! For me, the stark realization of this only fully comes home when I open the

A SEMANTIC VOYAGE?

Oxford English Dictionary (Volume VII) and find that its first entry under 'offering' is (the italics being mine):
1 a. The presenting of something to God . . . as an act of worship or devotion; sacrifice; oblation.
   b. The action of the verb *OFFER*, *in other senses: tender or presentation for acceptance,* for sale, etc.

and, under 'offer', it has (after two more 'neutral' paragraphs):
3. To present or tender for acceptance *or refusal*; to hold out (a thing) to a person to take *if he will (The prevailing sense).*

THE PREVAILING SENSE!!! But from whence? OED finds its *first* example in c.1375, followed by c.1400, 1548, 1596 (Shakespeare) and 1611, where the Bible (2 Sam. 24.12) is cited. Certainly there, *this* sense of 'offer' seems well justified by the Hebrew NOTEL 'ALEYKA='I lift/bear up/hold out over you . . .' But are we really to invest, e.g., Malachi 1.11 with this same nuance? And *a fortiori* are we to interpret the 'offertory procession' in the eucharist, or formulae like 'We offer you this bread and this cup' in the same way? That would not be merely the 'shallow and romantic Pelagianism' of Michael Ramsey's famous stricture—it would clearly be the full-blown, deep-seated British disease!

5. Some New Testament Pointers

It will be readily apparent that there is no space in a short essay to work out the ramifications of all this, nor to examine the sacrificial theology of the Scriptures themselves,[1] but one or two bald statements concerning the New Testament use of sacrificial language may perhaps indicate the centrality of the matter, at least.

First, I see least difficulty, on the face of it, about applying the 'prevailing sense' of 'offer' to Christ's own self-giving sacrifice, though this needs closer examination, and might raise more problems than it solves, especially as regards '. . . to take *if he will.'* Second, it is clear that there *are* things in the New Testament arguably linked, in some way, to the total eucharistic act, which the baptized believer *is* called upon to be giving sacrificially to God on his own account (e.g. praise, thanksgiving, faith, (financial) tribute, body etc.) The problem with the 'prevailing sense' of 'offer' here is that it may inadvertently introduce the nuance of 'doing God a favour', rather than rendering an obedient response to God's own 'favour'.

Thirdly, and crucially in the context of Dr. Williams's thesis, I repeat what I set out at some length in LS. 5. Any attempt to justify 'offer' language as corresponding to the *'poieite'* of the anamnesis rubric still

---

[1] The work of Robert J. Daly S.J. in *Christian Sacrifice* (Washington 1978) is a magisterial treatment of the spadework on this. In it he examines the question, 'Did the NT and the Early Church consider the Eucharist to be sacrificial?' He says that '. . . the Early Church did not consider the Eucharist to be a sacrifice.' but he concludes, '. . . that the N.T. Church considered the Lord's Supper and its own liturgical re-presentation of it to be . . . a sacrificial event.' I myself would prefer to talk about a cultic commemorative act *based on* a covenant-establishing sacrifice (see L.S. 5 p.27ff.), but I suspect that, if we could first nail the 'offer' business, we would not be very far apart.

seems to me (at best) entirely gratuitous. If it has to bear the weight of the 'prevailing sense' it becomes, in my estimation, positively tendentious.

6. The Next Stage?
It is, of course, perfectly obvious that Dr. Williams holds no such view, even remotely. The specimen citation, above, from his page 11 (even befogged, as it is for me, by the 'offer/offering' terminology) and its immediate context make this quite plain. Nor should my excursus be primarily regarded as a response to, much less a repudiation of, his main thesis. It is a *reaction*, but one, I trust, of which the relevance is apparent. My main argument is twofold, plus, I think, a pertinent tangential point.

To take the latter first. I am convinced that somewhere along the way a significant semantic 'leap' has occurred in the language of the debate. My own lexical studies point primarily to the Latin, but others may feel that it is the English 'prevailing sense' being 'read in' to the Latin that has caused the problem. If, however, it *is*, as I suspect, the Graeco-Roman philosophical propensity for the framework of physics and metaphysics, static and systematic analysis, individualism etc., and its consequent abstractions, that has occasioned the 'leap',—from the Semitic framework, with its integrated unitive view of reality expressed in pragmatic, dynamic and corporate terminology—then it suggests to me that it is possibly the category of 'metaphor' itself, defined in O.E.D. as 'Application of name or descriptive term to an object to which it is not literally applicable', that has occasioned the metamorphosis, and itself needs scrutiny!

However that is secondary. I am chiefly concerned to put two points to Dr. Williams. First, what does he feel about the implied view expressed here that the patristic sources themselves cannot be regarded as unquestioningly authoritative for the interpretation of the biblical material, but must themselves *be* scrutinized and assessed by a radical re-examination of the biblical evidence, and that therefore any attempted rehabilitation of the 'metaphor' (as he calls it) of sacrifice, including 'offer/offering' language, must be justified *on biblical grounds?*

Second, and most important of all, does he accept that the 'offer/offering' language is, given the 'prevailing sense', no longer tenable in this debate, and must now be eschewed, along with 'prevent' in the Prayer Book collects and 'indifferently' in the prayer for the Church militant, as words rendered useless by a dramatic change of meaning? If so, perhaps we can proceed towards the summit by taking our bearings from arguably less-loaded terms like 'bring near', 'present', 'render', 'set before', 'give', etc. Perhaps we could start with Malachi 1.11?

3. CHRIST'S PRIESTHOOD AND 'EUCHARISTIC SACRIFICE'— AN 'HISTORICAL' AXE TO A 'METAPHORICAL' ROOT?

by Christopher Hancock

Rowan Williams' Study *Eucharistic Sacrifice: The Roots of a Metaphor* is a penetrating, eirenical study of the patristic roots of a classic ecumenical *crux interretum*. But his sights are evidently set upon making his heavenly and metaphorical patristic exegesis, with its careful defence of Christ's agency in a 'eucharistc sacrifice', acceptable to sometimes over-sensitive Reformation sensibilities.[1] Without relinquishing altogether the patristic purview of his study, this response embraces consideration of some of the sixteenth century, and thence twentieth century, issues it raises. Rowan Williams has provided a timely re-interpretation of the eucharistic sacrifice, in a characteristic 'high' Anglican mode with its heavenly high-priestly perspective.[2] Since Christ's priesthood is a crucial feature of his argument the roots of its eucharistic association warrant careful historical examination, as illuminating in turn the Reformers' responses.

1. The Reformers' Reaction?

Spurning the dangers of speculation and drawn on by Rowan Williams' courteous approach to the Continental Reformers, we enquire: how would, say, Martin Luther and John Calvin have reacted? Would Dr. Martin, for example, have barked back, in a more theologized form, the sentiments expressed in *The Fortunes of Nigel*—'Metaphors are no arguments, my pretty maiden!'[3]— and discoursed on the real, once-for-all, sacrifice of Christ, at the heart of his *theologia crucis?* Or, would the pervasive humanist spirit he abhorred have affected his theology of the 'Word' to such an extent that he would have found sympathy in the use of 'metaphor',— particularly as interpreted by the literary critic John Middleton Murry 'Metaphor is as ultimate as speech itself, and speech as ultimate as thought'.[4] Would Calvin, the lawyer, have posited that Christ came to put an end to 'types' and 'metaphors'?; or Calvin, the pastor, have sympathized with the paranetical sections of Williams' essay, particularly regarding excessive Christian self-effacement?[5]

Clearly, to question their response is to expose not only the personal, but more importantly, the theological differences which sundered the sixteenth century Protestant Reformation. But, though this is an implicit indictment against Williams' generalized treatment of Reformation theology and a goad to analyse his *penchant* for Calvin, it is also a reminder of the undeniable division of Christendom since the Reformation, which no amount of well-motivated ecumenical

---

[1] See in particular his Introduction.
[2] For recognition of the prominence of Christ's heavenly high priesthood in anglo-catholic eucharistic thought, see A. M. Ramsey *From Gore to Temple* (London, 1960), pp.50-1; G. Aulen *Eucharist and Sacrifice* (Edinburgh, 1958), p.55; E. Scheller *Das Priesterthum Christi am Anschluss an den H. Thomas von Aquin* (Paderborn, 1934), p.371f.
[3] Quoted from S. McFague *Metaphorical Theology: Models of God in Religious Language* (S.C.M., London, 1982), p.32.
[4] *Ibid.*
[5] L.S. 31, p.27.

theological reductionism can traduce. What is more, however, in the very act of acknowledging a self-conscious movement of 'protest' in which the Reformers were at one, we are prompted by Sallie McFague's *Metaphorical Theology* (1982) to recognize in Luther's 'masks' of the revelation of God veiled in symbols, and Calvin's notion of divine 'accommodation', by which God stoops to our level by speaking in 'signs' and 'images', the fundamentally 'metaphorical' thrust inherent in Protestantism.[1] That Williams' enquiry ends in recognition of a 'metaphor' is not, of itself, something the Protestant Reformers would have opposed. Again, their concern for *sola Christi* is claimed to be a primary consideration in Williams' mind[2] whilst the heavenly perspective, viewing Christ's sacrifice and the eucharist *sub specie aeternitatis*, parallels, if it does not inspire, a sense of *sola dei gloria*. That the *sola scriptura* principle would have been satisfied is less likely, and more unlikely still omission of the limited responsive human element implicit in *sola fideism* at the heart of the Reformers' protest. What, though, of their responses to this particular presentation of the eucharistic sacrifice, and the place of Christ's priesthood in them?

. . . (a) Luther

Luther's informed repudiation of the Nominalist theory and popular practices of the Roman sacrificial Mass was reluctant in its conservatism, but ultimately decisive in its defensiveness towards the gospel principles *sola fidei: sola gratia*. He ultimately accepted that the sacrifice in the mass was limited to man's responsive self-giving in thanks and praise on the divine *beneficium* and *donum* in Christ's one atoning sacrifice on the Cross: not *sacrificium* but *testamentum*, Luther concluded.[3] So, in his *Treatise on the New Testament*, published in July of the critical year 1520, prior to the better-known *Babylonian Captivity of the Church*, he wrote: 'We would let the mass be a sacrament and a testament, and this is not and cannot be a sacrifice'.[3] But this apparent finality is then qualified in a remarkable passage, reflecting sympathy with a position akin to Williams':

'To be sure, this sacrifice of prayer, praise, and thanksgiving, and of ourselves, we are not to present before God in our own person, but we are to lay it on Christ and let him present it, as Paul teaches in Heb. 13: "Let us offer the sacrifice of praise to God continually, that is, the fruit of lips which confess him", and all this through Christ. For he is also a priest, as Psalm 110 says: "You are a priest forever after the order of Melchizedek"; because he intercedes for us in heaven, receives our prayer and sacrifice, and through himself, as a godly priest, makes them pleasing to God, as St. Paul says again in Heb. 9: "He is ascended into heaven to be a mediator in the presence of God for us . . .". From

---

[1] cf. esp. *ibid.* pp.32-42.
[2] cf. LS. 31, p.5.
[3] cf. V. Vatja *Luther on Worship* (ET, Philadelphia,1958), pp.39-40; and, on the connection between the sacrifice of Calvary and the eucharist in Luther, H. Sasse *This is my Body: Luther's Contention for the Real Presence in the Sacrament of the Altar*, (Minneapolis, 1959), pp.380, 382.
[4] M. Luther *Treatise on the New Testament*, in J. Pelikan and H. J. Lehmann (eds.) *Luther's Works*, 55 Vols., (Philadelphia, 1943) 35.99.

these words we learn that we do not offer Christ as a sacrifice, but Christ offers us. And in this way it is permissible, yea, profitable to call the mass a sacrifice, not on its own account, but because we offer ourselves as a sacrifice along with Christ, that is we lay ourselves on Christ by firm faith in this testament, and appear before God with our prayer, praise, and sacrifice only through him and through his mediation; and we do not doubt that he is our priest and minister in heaven before God. Such faith, forsooth, brings it to pass that Christ takes up our cause, presents us, our prayer and praise, and also offers himself for us in heaven. If the mass were so understood and therefore called a sacrifice it would be well'.[1]

But Luther added: 'Few understand the mass in this way. For they suppose that only the priest offers the mass as a sacrifice before God'.[2]

As it stands, this attempt to adduce heavenly roots, in the ascended priestly agency of Christ, for talk of the 'eucharistic sacrifice', suggests Reformation endorsement of Williams' interpretation. In the pressure of later controversy, however, regarding Romish eucharistic practices, the manner of Christ's presence, the immediacy of faith, and perfect finality of Christ's sacrifice on Calvary, Luther's opposition to 'massing' priests and eucharistic sacrifices clarified.[3] Significantly too, his later writings reveal reluctance to ascribe to Christ's heavenly priestly ministry anything other than a literal *oralis et vocalis* intercession.[4] It might be claimed Luther himself self-consciously 'immobilized' Christ as priest in heaven; there being in his persistent mediaeval priest-king dualism a radical distinction between the historical earthly priestly sacrifice on the cross, and the eternal heavenly intercession of Christ, the ascended, seated, priest-king. Certainly, Luther preserved the sense that Christ is 'priest and offering together', and this offering was eternal in its validity and effect. But the burden of Luther's emphasis fell upon the earthly focus of Christ's priestly ministry, so that, though he stresses Christ is 'not sitting idle in heaven', he gives, as Siggins points out, 'relatively minor treatment' to Christ's heavenly intercession, and we even see his prayer identified primarily with John 17, or Christ's words from the cross.[5]

Christology, soteriology, and sacramental theology, are interdependent in Luther's theology, and we cannot doubt that, in his maturer reflection, defence of the *'tetelestai'* in Christ's earthly sacrifice, and reserve regarding the nature of his heavenly priestly ministry, would have led Luther to oppose the reinterpretation of the eucharistic

[1] *Ibid.*
[2] *Ibid.* p.100.
[3] On the radical distinction between Luther's later thought and contemporary Roman Catholicism, see F. C. Clark *Eucharistic Sacrifice and the Reformation* (London, 1960), p.103: 'The Reformation hostility to the sacrifice of the altar is found to be connected in a coherent pattern with the basic Reformation doctrines of grace, of justification, of the Church and the sacraments, and ultimately of Christology'.
[4] cf. A. J. Tait *The Heavenly Session of our Lord* (London, 1912), p.163.
[5] cf. I. D. Kingston Siggins *Martin Luther's Doctrine of Christ* (New Haven and London, 1970), pp.118-9. On Christ 'the eternal high priest' in Luther's thought, see *ibid.* pp.46, 117-9, 121, 156.

sacrifice Williams suggests, and probably to endorse the 'one, once, once-for-all' spirit of much popular modern evangelical protestantism *vis-à-vis* Christ's 'sacrifice'. Luther's later stress upon the eucharist as *recollection* of one earthly event by Christ the one true sacrificing priest, not *reproduction* of an eternal heavenly action by him in the eucharist, is surely the basis of a 'Lutheran' response to Williams.

. . . (b) Calvin

Calvin, too, rejecting the eucharistic sacrifice as in any sense propitiation, repetition, or application of Christ's once-for-all sacrifice on the Cross, restricted the meaning of a eucharistic 'sacrifice' to that of a willing sacrifice of gratitude to God on the part of the communicants, offered in faith and charity by godly believers united in love to Christ and one another. Calvin's interpretation is shaped by his characteristic emphasis both upon the sacraments as the 'signs' of the mystical communion between Christ the Mediator and the Church of believers, and upon the work of the Holy Spirit, who unites us to Christ and everything he has of life in himself, and makes the flesh of Christ, though in heaven, our food—for the communion is for Calvin a heavenly meal. The ascended life and heavenly ministry of Christ, the priestly mediator and king in heaven, are of foundational importance for Calvin's sacramental theology. But Calvin's preparedness to discourse on heavenly matters derived from a particular view of biblical revelation not a 'Catholic' or patristic sacramentalism.

In contrast to Lutheran tradition, then, Reformed theology makes much of the eternal, active, heavenly ministry of Christ as 'priest'. Christ is, in Calvin, both the eternal priest-king and the sympathizing, heavenly priestly mediator.[1] As mediator he is eternally God and Man, the divine-human principle of cosmic unity, whose sacramental communion with man unites heaven and earth; and, though present everywhere according to his divinity—his human flesh being in heaven—Christ is present with his people in a special manner in this supper. But, such was Calvin's sense of the indivisible unity of the person of Christ that, not only does his belief in the whole Christ being present in his divinity lead him to suggest Christ is present—almost bodily present—on earth after the resurrection, but it also undergirds his stress upon the fundamental unity of Christ's earthly and heavenly ministry. For Calvin, Christ's priestly sacrifice and intercession are two parts of one whole, neither divisible nor, at times, distinguishable. Therefore, as Williams recognizes, not only is Christ's sacrifice accordingly of eternal efficacy, it is also, in his eternal heavenly intercession, an eternal 'heavenly sacrifice'. In the notion of a 'heavenly sacrifice' there is found in later Reformed tradition a sometimes remarkable linguistic affinity with more 'Catholic' eucharistic terminology, as is seen, for example, in some seventeenth century English Prebyterians, in the eucharistic hymns of the Wesleys, and in the theology of the Milligans in Scotland at the end of the nineteenth century. Reformed thought embraces various traditions emphasizing

---

[1] On Calvin's doctrine of Christ's priestly office, see J. F. Jansen *Calvin's Doctrine of the Work of Christ* (Edinburgh, 1956), Chapter 2 'The Offices of Christ in Calvin's Systematic Theology'.

the 'heavenly high-priestly perspective' characteristic of William's eucharistic viewpoint. They are patient of a variety of eucharistic theologies—from those accommodating a 'commemorative' eucharistic sacrifice, to those embodying fierce rejection of even the language of 'sacrifice' enjoined in a eucharistic context. Williams' stress upon the active agency of Christ, the living heavenly priest, in and over the eucharist, is one which Calvin and some Reformed writers would not have rejected.

But, if this analysis of the Reformers is correct, particularly regarding their very different understanding of Christ's heavenly priestly ministry, it now becomes pertinent to enquire—whence did these very different traditions derive? Are there, significantly, more and varied patristic roots than Williams' essay suggests?

2. What are the Roots of the Reformers' Responses?

Williams' composite approach is open to the charge of undue harmonization and the suspicion of this is aroused rather than quieted by his open admissions of terminological fluidity or hermeneutical complexity (cf. pp.18, 20). Study of the roots of the Reformers' responses, again particularly regarding Christ's heavenly priestly ministry, suggests that their divergences were antedated in the sub-apostolic and patristic eras if not in the apostolic age itself.

The Reformers' responses were rooted, firstly, in a common doctrinal and devotional adherence to the teaching of scripture, and, in particular, that of Hebrews—whence the language of 'priesthood' and 'sacrifice' in the Christian church most readily derived. Together with Romans, Hebrews was central to the Reformation protest: *The Apology of the Augsburg Confession* of 1530 even declared, 'Our cause is based primarily on the Epistle to the Hebrews'.[1] Luther lectured on Hebrews during the critical period embracing publication of the ninety-five theses, April 1517-March 1518, during which his basal convictions *solus Christus* and *iustitia dei passiva* were crystallized through recognition of the antithetical relation between the Old and New Testaments.[2] Despite its early importance for him, in his later years Luther's confidence in Hebrews, and thence perhaps to an extent his reserved treatment of Christ's heavenly priesthood, was vitiated by pre-occupation with its late canonical acceptance in the West and with Apollos' supposed authorship. As his lectures illustrate, too, however, Luther's exegesis of Hebrews' doctrine of Christ's priesthood was conducted in opposition to, or qualification of, mediaeval exegesis.[3] For example, he tacitly rejects the sacrificial eucharistic gloss put on Heb. 10.1-3 by Aquinas and Lyra, and quotes Chrysostom's interpretation in his gloss on Heb. 9.24, with a view to de-emphasizing the sacrificial character of the eucharist, which he restricts to the

---
[1] cf. *The Apology of the Augsburg Confession* (1530), Art. 24, Par. 53; quoted from F. Hildebrandt *I Offered Christ* (London, 1967), p.95.
[2] cf. K. Hagan *A Theology of Testament in the Young Luther. The Lectures on Hebrews* (Leiden, 1974), pp.9f, 59ff.
[3] cf. *ibid.* p.2.

church's daily spiritual sacrifice of itself to God.[1] In contrast to Luther, Calvin's *Commentary on Hebrews*, (1559), was the fruit of his mature reflection. It testifies to: (i) the centrality Christ's priesthood had come to occupy in Calvin's theology through its inherence in his fully-fledged doctrine of the *triplex munus Christi;* (ii) his adherence to Chrysostom's stress upon Christ's heavenly priesthood as expressive of his sympathetic suffering love; and, (iii) the traditional Western exegesis, traceable particularly from Justin and heavily dependent upon the Vulgate, which tended to identify closely Christ's sacrifice and intercession.[2] The present tense of the Vulgate of Hebrews 8.3—'Necesse *est* quod offerat'—supported a eucharistic theology of an heavenly offering which Calvin rejected, but his exegesis of the verse stressed both that Christ's priesthood 'is not earthly or carnal, but of a more excellent kind', and 'our prayers to be heard must be founded on sacrifice'.[3]

Thus there are deeper roots for the differences Luther and Calvin reflect: roots which go deeper still if we accept Frances Young's identification of Chrysostom's presentation of Christ's heavenly sympathizing priesthood as indicative of a characteristic feature of Antiochene theology,[4] so far removed in spirit from Luther's stress on Christ's heavenly kingship, but so near to an intercessory (*not* propitiatory) suffering in heaven, born of fellow-feeling with humanity. But recognition of an Eastern flavour to historic Calvinism is not new—both turned confidently and consistently to the teaching of Hebrews; both grounded Christ's priesthood in his incarnate sonship, and rejected (*pace* Athanasius v. the Arians) those who found talk of his priestly intercession subordinationist; both found in the priesthood of Christ endorsement of their incarnationist Christology, presenting Christ the 'priest', as man's representative and head. There is also a strand in Eastern patristic thought, for example in Clement of Alexandria, Theodoret, and Chrysostom himself, which subsumed Christ's heavenly priestly ministry beneath the fact of his presence in heaven. So, in Theodoret's *Commentary on Hebrews* we find: 'Now Christ is priest . . . not making an offering himself, but acting as the head of those who offer'.[5] No talk of Christ's heavenly priestly ministry in Eastern patristic thought—however much it stresses Christ's actively worshipping as priest 'with us', undergirding the church's sacrificial offering of praise, worship and sacrificial living in the eucharist (cf. Williams, p.33)—can deny that honouring immobilization of Christ in heaven, also found in many writers, eager to stress the power of Christ's passive incarnate presence in heaven, his offering on the cross behind him. It is surely this note of finality which Calvin, too, seeks to retain.

Finally, though, can we discern any patristic justification for the objections Luther made to the eucharistic sacrifice? Firstly, of course,

---
[1] cf. *ibid.* pp.112-3.
[2] cf. A. J. Tait *Heavenly Session,* pp.116f.
[3] J. Calvin *The Epistle of Paul the Apostle to the Hebrews,* D. W. and T. F. Torrance (eds.) (Edinburgh, 1963) pp.105-6; cf. also A. J. Tait *op. cit.,* p.128f., on Calvin's use of the ambiguous phrase Christ's 'one perpetual (*perennis*) sacrifice'.
[4] F. Young *The Use of Sacrificial Ideas in Greek Writers from the New Testament, to John Chrysostom* (Philadelphia, 1979), p.285f.
[5] Theodore: Migne, P.G. LXXX, 1774; cited in F. Hildebrandt *I Offered Christ,* p.31.

from the apostolic era onwards, clear, fundamental, and even geographically-determined, responses to the doctrine of Christ's priesthood, in relation to the eucharist, can be found. The silence of the *Didache, Hermas,* and *Apocryphal Gospels,* is as significant as the Clement passage where, Christ is designated 'the high priest of all our offerings'—which *might* pertain to the eucharist, though neither the context nor subsequent usage of 'offerings' necessitate this interpretation.[1] New Testament scholarship is equally divided about whether or not Clement and Hebrews reflect a common older tradition regarding Christ as priest. The natural assumption of knowledge of it, characteristic of Hebrews, and the problem of proving the dependence of Clement on Hebrews 1.14, which at points it appears to parallel[2], give weight to the conviction that the figure of Christ as '(high) priest' was not confined to the Judaeo-Christian, Hellenic, environment often associated with Hebrews and the figure of Melchizedek. What is more, whereas Hebrews presents Christ as the heavenly priest who sympathizes, Clement has that earthly perspective characteristic of Luther, 'the high priest who offers our gifts, the patron and helper in our weakness', and, 'It is through him that we look straight at the heavens above. Through him we see mirrored God's faultless and transcendent countenance, through him the eyes of our heart were opened. Through him our un-intelligent and darkened mind shoots up into the light'.[3] Of course, this was not an age of theological linguistic precision. However, the fact that Hebrews 3.1 ('The apostle and high priest of our confession') is often interpreted as an early liturgical creedal tradition,[4]— echoed, in Clement and later embodied in the liturgical formula 'through our high priest, Jesus Christ', which Jungmann (following Funk) associated particularly with the *Apostolic Constitutions* and *Prefaces* of the *Mozarabic Liturgies* of the Gallican type[5]—suggests an early Western tradition, which stressed Christ's priesthood independently of Hebrews, and, as in Hebrews and I Clement, without immediate eucharistic associations. The independence of Christ's priesthood from the eucharistic sacrifice and its prime association with Christ's earthly sacrifice and his mediation of intercession, appears to reflect that dualism which Luther sought increasingly to preserve regardless of his attitude towards Hebrews. This is not to deny the image of an 'altar in heaven' found in Irenaeus, but it is to claim that, looking for the 'roots' of the eucharistic 'sacrifice', particularly as presented by Williams, requires that the roots of the doctrine of Christ's priesthood be considered in East *and* West. When this is done, we are forced to acknowledge the complexity of the sources which the Reformers inherited and may have in different ways reflected.

Far from stilling the storms of controversy, however, regarding the eucharistic sacrifice, Williams has, albeit in an eirenical spirit, raised afresh the fundamental differences which divide a 'catholic' and a 'protestant' view of the past and present nature of the relation between God and the world and between Christ's earthly and heavenly work.

---

[1] For a discussion of this phrase, cf. J. Lawson *A Theological and Historical Introduction to the Apostolic Fathers* (New York, 1961), pp.45-6.
[2] For a discussion of the debate concerning their relation, cf. e.g. G. L Cockerill, 'Heb. 1.1-14, I Clem. 36.1-6 and the High Priest Title' in *J. B. L.* 97 (1978), pp.437-440.
[3] I Clem. 36.1-2.
[4] cf. e.g. O. Michel *Der Brief an die Hebräer* (Göttingen, 1975[7]), pp.172-3
[5] J. A. Jungmann *Die Stellung Christi im liturgischen Gebiet* (Münster, 1925), pp.127 211-233.

4. DOING THEOLOGY IN HEAVEN?
by Nicholas Sagovsky

Rowan Williams' Study perplexes because the issues that one expects to appear in a study on eucharistic sacrifice, issues focussing on the *ephapax* of Hebrews and the propitiatory nature of the mass, appear in the first paragraph and then almost totally disappear from view. It also intrigues because he clearly asserts that 'the whole tenor' of his study argues against any 'attrition of faith in an effective atonement', but he does not secure his position in the way a Reformed theologian would. For him, 'the point is that where we start, where we are on secure ground, is the corporate sense of a renewal of love, freedom, and prayer, and of intimacy with the source of our being and our value, growing out of the story of Jesus' life and death and resurrection' (p.31). It is this, not the *ephapax* of Hebrews, that secures his position; and that leads me to ask questions.

The introduction pinpoints three main areas about which objections to eucharistic sacrifice 'seem to crystallize'. Two of these he deals with very effectively. His Study speaks volumes against any interpretation of the eucharistic sacrifice which would tend to 'transfer the agency to church or priest and thus immobilize Christ'. God is not to be manipulated by man. Further, there can be no 'ideological grounding for a strongly hierarchical understanding of the relation of ministers and laity'. Whatever the understanding of eucharistic sacrifice, it will not do to see the offering of it as the prerogative of the clergy, putting them in some sense above the laity. But Williams handles less satisfactorily his own first objection: 'that any hint of the eucharist being *a* sacrifice fatally compromises the *ephapax* of the letter to the Hebrews; it undermines the all-sufficiency of the cross and so removes the ground of Christian assurance'.

In order to bring this issue into focus it is necessary to spend a little time reviewing the doctrine or doctrines of eucharistic sacrifice as received in the West.[1] The broad stream of Catholic teaching has insisted that the eucharist is not just properly *called* a sacrifice, but that it *is* truly a sacrifice, and that it propitiates God. As the canon from the Council of Trent put it, 'If anyone says that the sacrifice of the Mass is not a propitiatory sacrifice ... *anathema sit.*'[2] Within the Constitution on the Most Holy Sacrifice of the Mass, there are, however, some important balancing statements: 'In this divine sacrifice ... the same Christ who offered himself once in a bloody manner on the altar of the cross is contained and is offered in an unbloody manner... The victim is one and the same: the same now offers through the ministry of priests, who then offered himself on the cross; only the manner of offering is different.'[3] In the identity of priest and victim the two sacrifices are held together. The 'priority of Christ's agency' (to quote Williams) is assured—but propitiation remains.

Anglicans have gone as far as they can to meet this definition. Jeremy Taylor spoke of the sacrifice of the eucharist as 'in its proportion an

---
[1] For a careful statement of 'the current doctrine of the eucharistic sacrifice at the time of the Reformation', see F. Clark, *Eucharistic Sacrifice and the Reformation,* second edition (Oxford, 1967), pp.93-5.
[2] DS 1753.
[3] DS 1743.

instrument of applying the proper Sacrifice to all the purposes which it first designed', so that it is 'ministerially and by application an instrument propitiatory'.[1] Robert Wilberforce allowed that the eucharist could be called propitiatory, but only 'by reference to that one perfect propitiation upon the cross'.[2] Bishop Gore, though pleading for the language of propitiation to be restricted, had to acknowledge that 'the word propitiatory in a wider sense may be applied, and from the days of Origen has been applied, to the eucharist.'[3]

Nevertheless, this is not to deny that there can be, in Gore's phrase, 'no repetition of the sacrifice upon the cross'. In its insistence upon this point, encapsulated by the *ephapax* of Hebrews, Anglicanism stands securely in the protestant tradition, but still not so far from Roman Catholic teaching which insists that, 'If anyone says that the sacrifice of the Mass . . . detracts from . . . the most holy sacrifice which Christ accomplished on the cross, *anathema sit.*'[4] Both traditions remain at one in insisting on the 'priority of Christ's agency' in redemption, and the perfection of that redemption, but there remains a real issue between them as to the relation of the sacrifice of the cross and the sacrifice of the mass. That this is no chimera, but is of abiding importance for Christian assurance, and Christian proclamation, is surely clear. This is the issue Williams fails to grasp.

Williams' prime focus is not the *ephapax* of Hebrews but the 'priority of Christ's agency'. This concern leads him into some distortion when he says that 'the basic theological premise in the classical Reformed thesis is the eternal saving agency of Christ which never needs to be "reawakened" or "applied" by human agents' (p.4). It would be more accurate, I suggest, to speak of the *ephapax,* the 'once-for-allness' of Calvary, as the basis of the Reformers' resistance to distortions in the sacrificial understanding of the eucharist—Christ ever-living to intercede certainly, but known to us in particular as mediator by virtue of his perfect and total self-giving in his death on the cross. This can be illustrated from Williams' chosen Reformers, Calvin and Jewel.

The nub of Calvin's objection to the sacrifice of the mass is that it is an insult to the priesthood of Christ, as though that priesthood had been ineffectually exercised when he gave himself in sacrifice. For him, 'the practice of daily sacrificing is inconsistent with and wholly foreign to the priesthood of Christ.'[3] The priest cannot offer such sacrifice for four reasons: because 'Christ alone was fit to offer himself'; because 'the Apostle asserts Christ's sacrifice to have been once offered, so that it is impious to repeat it'; thirdly, 'the Apostle acknowledges no sacrifice without blood and death'; lastly, 'the Apostle in speaking of obtaining pardon for sins, bids us flee to that one sacrifice which Christ offered on the cross, and makes this distinction between us and the fathers,

---

[1] Quoted in P. E. More and F. L. Cross eds., *Anglicanism* (London, 1962), p.495.
[2] R. I. Wilberforce, *The Doctrine of the Holy Eucharist* (London, 1853), p.350.
[3] C. Gore, *The Body of Christ* (London, 1901), p.177.
[4] DS 1754.
[5] J. Calvin, *Commentaries on the Epistle of Paul the Apostle to the Hebrews,* translated by J. Owen (Calvin Translation Society, Edinburgh, 1853), p.230.

that the rite of continually sacrificing was done away by the coming of Christ.'[1] All these objections focus on the cross as the specific guarantee of what is, admittedly, 'the priority of Christ's agency'. Calvin argues, against the Roman Catholic priesthood, that Christ is the perfect priest because he has performed his earthly work of atonement perfectly. Nevertheless, he is also concerned to set Christ's earthly work in the context of his eternal heavenly role: 'He died on earth but the virtue and efficacy of his death proceeded from heaven.'[2] It is in heaven that Christ now performs his priestly work of intercession. These two aspects of Christ's priestly office, the earthly and the heavenly, Calvin carefully holds together.

The same is true of Jewel. Williams quotes a passage which speaks of the one sacrifice as 'everlasting', relating 'that one sacrifice once offered' to 'our daily sacrifice'.[3] In the same section Jewel argues, 'The old fathers call that the daily sacrifice that Christ made once for all upon the cross, for that, as Christ is a priest for ever, so doth the same his sacrifice last for ever; not that it is daily and really renewed by any mortal creature, but that the power and virtue thereof is infinite in itself, and shall never be consumed.' Again, the discussion is linked indissolubly with the cross, and it is the *efficacy* of the sacrifice which is eternal, not the offering or accomplishing of it.

I do not find this to be true of Williams' Study, in which he seems in part to be reacting against a protestant theology that is in its turn unbalanced. He apologizes for Catholic defenders of 'eucharistic sacrifice' who have 'caricatured' Reformed doctrine 'as if it implied that our present salvation were a long-range effect of an event in the past' (p.4). Here I see no need to apologize. As the writer of Hebrews wrestles with the historicity and the transcendence of the cross, this is precisely how he, and so the Reformers, approach the sacrifice of Christ: as a once-for-all event in the past, which is dynamically effective today in and through the unchanging ministry of Jesus. To lose this is to lose a central dynamic of an incarnational religion which transforms the standing of man by making him a 'liturgical being' and raising up to heaven, but also brings the sharp light of heaven to focus on the dark places of the earth.

Here I think we have it. William's describes himself as exploring 'some of the mist-shrouded lower-levels' where the language of eucharistic sacrifice may be used with less conceptual clarity than in the great Reformation debates, but where we may rediscover what it means to 'think through the experience of renewed humanity in symbols'. At this level, he finds the sacrificial metaphor enormously fruitful: 'I have argued in this essay for a retrieval of the idea that the effect of Christ's sacrifice is to make us 'liturgical' beings, capable of offering ourselves, our praises and our symbolic gifts to a God who we know will receive us in Christ.' (p.27) All this makes good sense if we change the metaphor and think of Williams 'doing theology in heaven'.

[1] *ibid.*, p.233.
[2] *ibid.*, p.182.
[3] J. Jewel, *Reply to Harding's Answer*, in *The Woks of John Jewel, Bishop of Salisbury*, edited by J. Ayre (Parker Society, Cambridge, 1845), volume 1, p.128; quoted ES, p.4.

DOING THEOLOGY IN HEAVEN?

He comments himself on the closeness of the throne/altar themes, and his writing constantly puts me in mind of the text from Ephesians: 'In union with Christ Jesus (God) raised us up and enthroned us with him in the heavenly realms' (Eph. 2.6, NEB). Is it this heavenly context that allows the freedom of movement between the metaphors of offering: God offering Christ, Christ offering his blood, Christ offering the believer, the believer offering Christ? Such imaginative freedom seems to render much of the historical argument otiose.

This construction makes sense of Williams' starting with 'the corporate sense of a renewal of love, freedom, and prayer, and of intimacy with the source of our being and value'. As an account of worship, differs from what Williams refers to as Cranmer's 'recapitulation of the conversion experience' in the eucharist. Williams' whole approach stresses the celebration of our eucharistic communion in the risen Christ, rather than our communion in his death. The crucifixion has become the supposition for a corporate life 'hid with Christ in God', part of the 'story', which is the seed-bed for our present Christian experience. He begins from 'the effect of Christ's offering', which is 'to make us capable of offering, to count us worthy to stand and serve as priests'.

Perhaps we could express the difference between this approach and the approach against which the Reformers protested as the difference between theology done on earth and theology done in heaven. For Williams, the cross remains very obviously the gateway to heaven. As he has written elsewhere, 'Where there is salvation, its name is Jesus; its grammar is the cross and the resurrection.'[1] For the medieval Roman church the understanding of the cross was locked into earthly metaphore of cause and effect that focussed upon the agency of the priest and the transformation of the bread and wine. However much it produced 'nagging at God', it provided for a strong doctrine of assurance in and through the eucharistic presence. The breakdown of that assurance as its manifold inadequacies were revealed is the story of the Reformation. New avenues of assurance were to be found.

This is what, it seems to me, Williams presupposes. For those who can start with a 'corporate sense of a renewal of love, freedom, and prayer' (and there are many) well and good, but this will not do for a Luther, and it will not do for those who need some more 'objective' focus for their permitted sense of 'intimacy' with God. The cross as event, as pledge, as ground of hope is the symbolic assurance that this 'sense' is no delusion, but sober reality, a reality, we explore in metaphoric terms. It is at this point that I believe Williams' stimulating and creative study lacks balance. I would not drag him back again to the heartland of debates about propitiation. By his silence he shows the extent to which the application of logic to metaphoric statement can be misleading. However, I believe there is also a case to be made for a more 'earthbound' theology of the cross. I would ask of him if he has in this Study made as thoroughgoing an application as he might of his own fine words, when he wrote that 'The final control and measure and irritant in Christian speech remains the cross'.[2]

[1] R. Williams, *Resurrection* (London, 1982), p.72.
[2] R. Williams, *The Wound of Knowledge* (London, 1979), p.3.

5. EUCHARISTIC SACRIFICE—WHAT CAN WE LEARN FROM CHRISTIAN ANTIQUITY?

by Kenneth Stevenson

Anglican Background

The 1966 controversy in the Church of England over the words, 'we offer this bread and this cup', was no merely internal Anglican affair, but it showed that many Anglicans are happy with sacrificial language in the eucharist. Many reasons can be given, and in a series of articles in *Theology* at the time, four scholars made some observations on this difficult subject, among whom was Geoffrey Cuming, who marshalled a variety of seventeenth century evidence to support the legitimacy of 'we offer this bread and this cup' as an authentic Anglican formulation.[1] Moreover, many Christians are ready to accept the 'metaphor' of sacrifice in relation to the eucharist, whether through study of history, or because of the numerous eucharistic hymns which are now part of the repertoire of countless congregations, including (let it be noted) many of Reformed traditions. Indeed, from the heart of the Lutheran tradition, the nineteenth century Danish hymn-writer, Nikolai Grundtvig is able to describe the eucharist as 'takkesangens offerskaal', a difficult formulation to translate exactly (perhaps translation looms much larger in this controversy than we ever imagine?), but which points to the eucharist as a spiritual sacrifice.[2]

Nonetheless, sacrificial language is anathema to many other Anglicans, who feel (many of them fervently) that *any* such language runs the risk of undermining Calvary. This takes us to the sixteenth century; Luther put asunder 'sacrament' and 'sacrifice'; Calvin distinguished between 'latreutical' and 'propitiatory' sacrifice (he was happy with the former, but not the latter); and Zwingli went the whole way and drove a wedge between 'remembrance' and 'sacrifice'. Zwingli's influence on the subsequent *piety* of the Reformed traditions was (arguably) greater than that of Calvin. Many of the opponents of 'we offer this bread and this cup' are, perhaps, Zwinglian (rather than Lutheran or Calvinist) in their theological stand-point, and it is easy to see in the progression from Luther to Zwingli how much more negative is the latter in reaction to the theology, liturgy, and spirituality of the late Mediaeval West.

Language *does* matter, especially in a Church (like ours) which expects its ordained clergy to swear oaths about what forms of worship are to be used in local congregations. And one of the problems in recent years is that the concept of theological pluralism has become a reality among laity in the parishes; you only have to be an itinerant celebrant or preacher to see abundant evidence for this, whether in the printed

---

[1] G. J. Cuming, 'The English Rite: "We offer this Bread and this Cup"', 4 *Theology* 69 (1966) pp.447-452.

[2] *Den Danske Salmebog,* Kobenhavn, 1953, no. 247 (I al sin glans nu straler solen', from stanza 5, which is laden with the theme of eucharistic praise; 'takke-sangens offerskal' means literally 'thanksong's drink-offering' ('skal' being also the traditional Danish drinking-greeting); I am indebted to Knud Ottosen, Lecturer in Church History, Arhus University, for drawing my attention to this hymn. On the place of Grundtvig in the nineteenth century, and in a wider perspective, see A. M. Allchin, *The Kingdom of Love and Knowledge* (D.L.T. 1979) pp.71-89 (on p.79 Allchin translates the formula as 'the sacrificial cup of thanksgiving').

version of ASB Rite A (or whatever), or the selection of hymns and songs most commonly used. The matter is even further complicated by the fact that in the last run-up to 1980, the section in Rite A which many of us call the 'offertory' was loosened up considerably[1], many churches use the Roman Catholic offertory prayers, and supporters of 'we offer this bread and this cup[1], some who did not get what they wanted for the anaphora in the years of labour on Revision Committees, can take liberties at the offertory as a kind of consolation-prize.[2]

Colin Buchanan himself has recently observed, with some obvious lamentation, how the real *theological* discussion never really happened[3], whether between Evangelicals and Anglo-Catholics, or between those two groups and the Liberals in the less fattening centre. It is, indeed, a pity that, precisely when ARCIC 'Statements' were being thrashed out, and world-wide ecumenism was addressing itself to these, and other related issues, the Liturgical and Doctrine Commissions did not sit down together for a dialogue including the origin of the metaphor of sacrifice in the early liturgies.[4] Doctrine Commissions, especially Anglican ones, ignore liturgical issues at their peril.

Patristic Liturgy
The New Testament is not the Book of Common Prayer of the early Church, although recent scholarship tends to maximize (rather than minimize) the liturgical context of much of the material, whether in the gospels, or elsewhere. Nonetheless, when it comes to describing the eucharist, the language used is primarily that of meal-fellowship, solidarity with the present Christ, and memorial. The sacrifice is that of Calvary, in the various ways interpreted by the gospel-writers, and the writers of the epistles, including Hebrews, which makes much of the eternal offering of Christ, and his place at the right hand of the Father.

But where else is the sacrifice? Many scholars, whether or not they would go to the stake for 'we offer this bread and this cup', see the sacrificial language of the early Church as emanating from late Jewish piety, which *spiritualized* sacrifice.[5] This is, therefore, a legitimate development, resulting from the diaspora (people cannot get to the temple so easily), prophetic warnings about the need for sacrificial living (worship and life should stand in direct relation), and the self-oblation of the worshipper to his God (the spirituality, above all, of the Psalter); further, the destruction of the temple posed even greater

[1] For an Evangelical interpretation of this issue, see Colin Buchanan, *The End of the Offertory—An Anglican Study* (Grove Liturgical Study 14), Grove Books, 1978).
[2] But see 'we bring before you this bread and this cup' in Eucharistic Prayer 3 (is 'bring' much different from *propheromen*'?).
[3] Colin Buchanan, 'Liturgical Revision in the Church of England in Retrospect', in Kenneth Stevenson (ed.), *Liturgy Reshaped* (S.P.C.K., 1982) p.154.
[4] See my forthcoming *Eucharist and Offering: A Liturgical Study*, . . . see also my '"Anaphoral Offering": Some Observations on Eastern Eucharistic Prayers' in *Ephemerides Liturgicae* 94 (1980), pp.209-228; and 'Eucharistic Offering: does research into origins make any difference?', in *Studia Liturgica* 15 (1982/3), pp.87-103 (=*La Maison-Dieu* 154 (1983), pp.81-106, French tr.).
[5] R. J. Daly, *Christian Sacrifice: The Judaeo-Christian Background before Origen* (Catholic University of America, Washington, 1978) *passim*.

questions for early Christians, with the cessation of its elaborate cult. Behind all this, too, are the important recent studies on the Jewish background of the liturgy. Jewish origins do not of themselves legitimize something, though Jewish spirituality is at the heart of the Eastern marriage rites (whereas the Latin West concentrated on the pagan Roman emphasis on the bride's change of state).[1] Jewish origins do, however, show that the *berakah*, the act of blessing, was understood to be sacrificial, in a spiritual sense; and the 'spiritual sense' is not 'abstract', but has a reality of its own.[2] From this wide starting-point, then, I would argue that the eucharist (though by no means the only activity of the early Church!) has a sacrificial character from the very start. To offer 'spiritual sacrifices' (1 Pet. 2.5) would, on this basis, include the eucharist, but also *all* Christian worship; (in the fourth century, John Chrysostom described *preaching* as a sacrificial act[3]); but the spiritual sacrifices spill over into acts of charity, service, support, and what we would nowadays call a 'Christian life-style'. In the *Didache* (14)[4], we find an early description of the whole eucharist as a sacrifice:

'. . . come together, break bread, and give thanks, having first confessed your transgressions, that your sacrifice may be pure'.

It goes on to explain the need for reconciliation in the Christian fellowship, the famous quotation from Mal. 1.11 (but deleting the reference to incense) follows next. Some would regard this as the foundation on which to build a Mediaeval Western view of the eucharist, whereas others would point out that *Didache* is not canonical, and includes the language of sacrifice because some parts of the early church had little choice, because sacrifice was so much part of the ancient world. I suggest a third interpretation, which would regard sacrifice already by the time of the *Didache* as a *necessary* view of the eucharist, because it best expressed the Christian insight that worship presupposes a sacrificial disposition on the part of the worshipper. We do not repeat Calvary; but we do its commemoration in a sacrificial frame of mind, and that gives to the *whole* celebration a sacrificial flavour. For *Didache,* the metaphor is essential, though not explicitly developed.

The early non-liturgical evidence has been discussed elsewhere by Richard Hanson and Rowan Williams,[5] and since my task is confined to

[1] See my *Nuptial Blessings: A Study of Christian Marriage Rites* (Alcuin Club Collections 64, S.P.C.K., 1982) (=Oxford University Press, New York, 1983).
[2] T. J. Ledogar, *Acknowledgement: Praise-Verbs in the Early Greek Anaphora,* (Herder, Rome, 1968) pp.99ff.; see also J. Laporte, *La doctrine eucharistique chez Philon d'Alexandria* (Théologie Historique 16) (Beauchesne, Paris, 1972).
[3] *Hom. in Rom.* 29.1.
[4] Text in R. C. D. Jasper/G. J. Cuming (ed.), *The Prayers of the Eucharist: Early and Reformed* (Oxford University Press, New York, 1980) pp.15f.; see also T. J. Talley, 'The Eucharistic Prayer of the Ancient Church According to Recent Research: Results and Reflections' in *Studia Liturgica* 11 (1976), pp.146ff.
[5] R. P. C. Hanson, *Eucharistic Offering in the Early Church* (Grove Liturgical Study 19, Grove Books, 1979); Rowan Williams, *Eucharistic Sacrifice—The Roots of a Metaphor* (Grove Liturgical Study 31, Grove Books 1982). To these should be added the important recent study of John D. Laurance, 'Le président de l'Eucharistie selon Cyprien de Carthage: un nouvel éxamen' in *La Maison-Dieu* 154 (1983), pp.151- 165, in which the traditional view of Cyprian as 're-offering Christ' is challenged and a fresh interpretation of the evidence is provided.

EUCHARISTIC SACRIFICE—WHAT CAN WE LEARN FROM CHRISTIAN ANTIQUITY?

the liturgical material, we now leap on in time (though, in my view, not that much), to the (Syriac) anaphora of Addai and Mari,[1] which may well be third century (if not earlier). Strongly Semitic in character, it keeps that imprecise metaphor of the whole eucharist as sacrificial: 'You, O Lord, in your unspeakable mercies make a gracious remembrance . . . in the commemoration of the body and blood of your Christ which we offer to you upon the pure and holy altar . . . .'
'May he come, O Lord, your Holy Spirit and rest upon this oblation of your servants . . . for the pardon of debts . . .'
What is offered? The *commemoration* of Christ's death. What is prayed for? The presence of the Spirit on the *whole* eucharist. This language need alarm no protestant, as it is faithful to precisely those issues which became writ large more than a millennium later. It is in Hippolytus[2] that the first formula is replaced by 'we offer you the bread and the cup', whereas the second formula (the epiclesis) reappears, though with prayer for the unity of the church. The new first formula occurs in that part now termed the anamnesis, and it may be a later strand of the tradition behind this anaphora, indeed forming part of a unit consisting of the institution-narrative and the anamnesis which were inserted into the older core of thanksgiving-series and supplication (epiclesis).[3]

The explicit offering of the bread and cup has not (so far) appeared in the liturgy and it is here worth pointing out that there are many more problems associated with this anaphora than most people allow, so that the narrative-anamnesis may not, in fact, be authentic third century material. Nonetheless, such an offering occurs in the (fourth century) West-Syrian/Byzantine tradition, in the anaphoras of Basil, Chrysostom, and James.[4] The offering of 'gift' lies already in the background in the writings of Clement, Justin, and Irenaeus,[5] but I would see this as secondary, both in chronology *and* theological priority, to the view of the whole celebration being an offering, in bringing together the One Offering of Christ, and the offering of the worshippers, in a spiritual sacrifice. Moreover, the offering word in the Latin translation of Hippolytus is 'offerimus', corresponding probably to the (original) Greek 'prospheromen'; the relative weakness of this verb in the available sacrificial vocabulary is perhaps surprising, for nowhere do we find the full-blooded 'thusiazo' ('sacrifice'). Another important feature of the Hippolytan text is that the offering-verb comes *before* any petition for sanctification or consecration of the eucharist, of the people, or of the elements; and this order of anamnesis-offering-epiclesis is studiously adhered to as an essential part of eucharistic logic in the Greek anaphoras; many Syriac ones (as we shall see) have a corresponding

---

[1] Text in B. D. Spinks (ed.), *Addai and Mari—The Anaphora of the Apostles: A Text for Students* (Grove Liturgical Study 24, Grove Books, 1980) pp.14ff.
[2] Text in G. J. Cuming, *Hippolytus—A Text for Students* (Grove Liturgical Study 8, Grove Books, 1976) p.11.
[3] L Ligier, 'Célébration divine et anamnèse dans la première partie de l'anaphore ou canon de la messe orientale', in *Eucharisties d'Orient et d'Occident*, II, (Editions du Cerf, Paris, 1970) pp.139-178.
[4] See texts in Jasper/Cuming, *op. cit.*, pp.101, 90, and 63.
[5] See Hanson, *op. cit.*, pp.6ff.

offering at the intercession, instead of the anamnesis; and Greek Mark (Coptic) and John Son of Thunder (Ethiopic) have a different structure altogether.[1] The function, however, of offering-verbs in the Eastern anaphoras repays careful study. Unlike the Roman Canon, offering-language is but one theme, lying under the surface of the central features, such as thanksgiving, reconciliation, and supplication for the gift of the Spirit in the celebration (epiclesis) and the life of the Church and the world (intercession). And, as Robert Taft has recently shown, the later Byzantine 'Great Entrance' is no offertory-procession (as Westerners have consistently mis-understood it) but the solemn transfer of the gifts from the prothesis to the holy table.[2] The evolution of the Eastern anaphoras (as I have shown elsewhere)[3] is a far more subtle and complex affair when it comes to offering. For example, the past-tense verb 'proethekamen' (='we presented')—i.e. presented *before* the anaphora—occurs in the early fragment of the anaphora of Basil, an antecedent of the one used by the Coptic Church today. Is this past tense, and neutral verb, an 'Egyptian symptom', borrowed from Greek Mark, where it also appears? Or is it an authentic original, from Cappadocia, perhaps an archetype, used by Basil as a young man, but forming the basis of his more extensive re-working later in his life? These (and other) questions are more than literary—they are theological, because the ideas and the nuances and the emphases alter noticeably within the Basil anaphoras, so that by the time we reach the Byzantine version (used in the Byzantine rite[4] on festivals), praise is 'offered' in the 'preface', the bread and wine are 'memorials of his saving passion . . . which we have set forth' before the institution-narrative, and the link between memorial (anamnesis) and supplication (epiclesis and intercession) is made not by a present-tense verb, 'we offer', but by a participle ('offering')[5], which was subsequently changed to 'we offer', in line with Chrysostom and James. This bevy of offering-material is formulated in order to spell out the 'sacrifice of praise'-character of the eucharist (preface), but also that the eucharist is a memorial-sacrifice (anamnesis). Moreover, the Eastern anaphoras repeatedly use offering-language at the *intercessions*, usually including those who have offered the gifts (i.e. the congregation), extending the character of *self-oblation*, the background of all true intercession.[6]

---

[1] See text of Mark in Jasper/Cuming, *op. cit.*, pp.48f. and John Son of Thunder in A. Hänggi/I. Pahl (ed.), *Prex Eucharistica* (Spicilegium Friburgense 12), (Fribourg University Press, 1968) pp.153ff.; an appeal to the Greek West Syrian/Byzantine logic is made by T. J. Talley, 'The Eucharistic Prayer: Tradition and Development', in *Liturgy Reshaped*, pp.62f, from an Anglican standpoint in the Caroline-Scottish/American Liturgy tradition.

[2] R. F. Taft, *The Great Entrance* (Orientalia Christiana Analecta 200, Pontifical Institute of Oriental Studies, Rome, 1975) pp.257-275.

[3] See articles cited above, p.27, note 4.

[4] Compare texts in Jasper/Cuming, *op. cit.*, pp.34ff. (later Coptic Basil for first part of anaphora, followed by complete text of fragment of early Coptic: but I find the translation of *'proethēkamen'* as 'we have set forth' inadequate, and prefer to render it as a past-historic/aorist); compare this with later Byzantine, pp.98ff.

[5] Hippolytan forms recur in many denominations today.

[6] On the sacrificial character of intercession, see my ' "Ye Shall Pray For": The Intercession', in *Liturgy Reshaped*, pp.32-47.

EUCHARISTIC SACRIFICE—WHAT CAN WE LEARN FROM CHRISTIAN ANTIQUITY?

Observations and Suggestions

Memorial-sacrifice is a theme which recurs among the classical Anglican divines, and it originates from a mentality which finds no difficulty in linking together what Zwingli tried to drive apart.[1] The memorial *is* the celebration, the whole eucharist, focused on what the faithful are doing, namely giving thanks over bread and wine, and sharing them together in the presence of God. The 'offering' in the anamnesis is only a way of bringing together the memorial-language ('remembering . . .') and the supplication-language (the epiclesis). But the memorial-sacrifice is not *confined* to those 'formulae' at the anamnesis, because it is a description of the whole eucharist, in which thanks and praise are offered for the work of God in Christ, the worshippers offer themselves in the eucharist (epiclesis and intercession, whether the latter comes in the anaphora or elsewhere in the liturgy). Two important points, however, need to be made. First, although the formulation 'remembering . . ., we offer' is part of the tradition of the Roman Canon and the three Byzantine anaphoras, it is by no means universal in the East, for we find that the reticence and imprecision of Addai and Mari persists in most of the anaphoras of the Syriac traditions represented today by the Syrian Jacobite and Maronite churches; and the Armenian anaphoras show similar tendencies.[2] These variegated eucharistic texts happily offer praise and supplication and intercession, and sometimes adopt deliberately paradoxical language in describing the work of Christ, but they seem almost to avoid saying 'we offer' at the anamnesis; and this may well witness to an ancient Semitic sensitivity which sees the eucharist as a spiritual sacrifice but is reluctant to be too specific about it.

Secondly, although many liturgies down the ages (not just Eastern ones) indulge in heavenly language of a high priestly kind, none of them appears to be precise about *how* the eucharist relates to the work of Christ in his intercession at the Father's right-hand. Both in that part of the anaphora which leads up to the Sanctus and in extended forms of anamnesis[3] which catalogue everything that Christ did (and still does), language, however rich, stops short of saying how the eucharist relates to this, other than that it joins in the heavenly liturgy of eternal praise (Sanctus) and intercession (anamnesis-epiclesis-intercession). And yet this is the fertile ground on which ARCIC and Lima 'Statements' grow some fruit which looks both ancient *and* modern![4] In a recent study of the issues in Reformed-Roman Catholic ecumenical dialogue about the eucharist, Alasdair Heron (no betrayer of Reformation principles, as his

---
[1] See G. Wagner, *Der Ursprung der Chrysostomusliturgie* (Liturgiewissenschaftliche Quellen und Forschungen 59, Aschendorff, Münster, 1973) pp.109ff.
[2] See articles cited above, p.27, note 4.
[3] See article in *Studia Liturgica* cited in n. 6 above, p.29; see also R. F. Taft, 'Historicism Revisited' in *Studia Liturgica* 14 (1982), pp.102f. and nn., where, following Jungmann, Taft notes the influence of Arianism.
[4] See text of 'Lima' liturgy in Colin Buchanan, *ARCIC and Lima on Baptism and Eucharist* (Grove Worship Series 86, Grove Books, 1983), pp.21f., (latter part of anaphora, and remarks by Buchanan, pp.12f.). The anamnetic formula, 'united in Christ's Priesthood, we present to you this memorial' seems to feel for a Syriac-sounding symbolism; see below, p.32, note 2.

book shows), queries Calvin's radical separation of 'remembrance' in the eucharist and the 'self-offering' of Christ:

'To put it at its sharpest, is there not a valid sense in which it is always and only *the sacrifice of Christ himself* that we set forth and hold out to the Father, because he has so identified himself with us that we are united with him? This union lies at the heart of Calvin's theology, but when it comes to the controversial matter of the sacrifice of the Mass he is so anxious to avoid any idea of repeating or adding to Christ's sacrifice that he also seems to rule out our *participation* in his self-offering. Our offering becomes simply a response—response *to* him rather than sharing *with* him in his offering, not only *or himself for us*, but *of us with himself.*'[1]

Heron goes on to suggest, moreover, that the work of Christ 'is at the same time the sanctifying and offering of our sinful human nature to God', and that the eucharist, as part of this work, 'is both a *receiving* of Christ as the Father's gift to us and a *sharing* in his offering to the Father of our nature, indeed of us.'[2] Here, perhaps, may lie an important means whereby an old deadlock may be broken; and the eucharist assume an entirely healthy Christology. Frances Young has recently argued that sacrifice, though exclusively a metaphor in modern parlance, is rich and vibrant as a vehicle for spiritual values, and as a Methodist, she comes from a tradition whose hymnody is rich and vibrant in the language of eucharistic sacrifice.[3] If we put Heron's searching for a theologically adequate solution to the question together with Young's insistence that the sacrificial understanding of life in Christ is just as 'relevant' as it was in the early centuries, then we do indeed have a way forward which keeps Calvary at the centre, but gives the eucharistic church its proper place as onlooker and beneficiary, and at the same time as caught up into the life of Christ who draws all men and women to himself. The ancients had different problems but the *eucharistic* developments in the three anaphoras of Basil are just as important as the Christological/Trinitarian ones; and the study of liturgy is only a limited affair when it is confined to cataloguing formulae. Nonetheless, the formulae of the ancient (and less ancient) East do demonstrate both variety in emphasis and sensitivity to fundamentals.

Problems persist today, even though much head-way has been achieved, by the grace of God. New Roman eucharistic prayers are composed on Eastern (and ancient Western) models, so that Roman Catholics will in time digest this liturgy into a piety that is not nearly so exclusively sacrificial' as that of a bygone era.[4] Churches of the

---

[1] A. Heron, *Table and Tradition: Towards an Ecumenical Understanding of the Eucharist*, (Handsel Press, Edinburgh, 1983), p.169.

[2] *ibid.* p.170; compare the 1982 *Scottish Liturgy*, 'Made one with him, we offer you these gifts and with them ourselves, a single, holy, living sacrifice' (pp.8f.) Heron, in correspondence with the writer, agrees wholeheartedly with the identification of this theological insight in the Episcopalian liturgy. Presbyterians and Episcopalians are not, after all, so far apart! (I am indebted to Dr. Gian Tellini, one of the drafters of the liturgy, for help on the background of this rite.)

[3] F. Young, *Sacrifice and the Death of Christ* (S.P.C.K., 1975) (=S.C.M. 1984).

[4] In the Spring of 1983, I was a Visiting Professor at the University of Notre Dame, Indiana, U.S.A., where my duties included delivering a series of lectures on

[continued on p.33 opposite

EUCHARISTIC SACRIFICE—WHAT CAN WE LEARN FROM CHRISTIAN ANTIQUITY?

Reformation lose their sensitivity about 'offertory', and even about some of the traditional 'offering' language in the body of the eucharistic prayer. But of the 'offertory', there must be some hesitations; to make it into a 'eucharistic-sacrificial *substitute*' runs many risks, even though the 'itch' to say something when the gifts are prepared can be for many presidents (and not just 'catholic' ones) irresistible. Our ecological approach to the eucharist, which places emphasis on the gifts *as* gifts, and the increasing view of anthropologists that the eucharist is a kind of sacrifice through its very character of being a solemn ritual meal—these, and many other factors prevent the eucharist from degenerating into a clinical exercise in which everything is so neatly defined that the whole game might as well be played from a computer print-out. That holds good of sacrifice, too, for one of the most important reasons for the viability of the metaphor of sacrifice today is that it speaks fundamentally about the *serious nature* of the Supper of the Lord at a time when there is a danger of 'eucharist and chips' setting in as a popular mentality, and, in words borrowed from the *Didache,* the 'sacrifice becomes impure'. Far from characterising a triumphalistic view of the church, the eucharistic sacrifice rather points to its poverty, and its complete dependence on Christ.

What, then, can Christian antiquity teach us? It cannot teach us everything. We live in a quite different age, and so we must beware of patristic fundamentalism in liturgy as much as biblical fundamentalism in theology. But it *can* teach us that the sacrificial metaphor is an important part of the eucharistic vocabulary, provided that it takes its place alongside the others, which include celebration, reconciliation, Spirit, and Kingdom. It can also teach us that we are on firmer ground when the liturgy, so far from consisting of a series of 'magic moments',[1] comprises of a sequence of significant features of sacrifice, particularly in the offering of praise and supplication, and, in so doing, offering the aspirations of the congregation in its life of faith to the living God. It can even teach us that the presentation of God's own things from God's own creation'[2] in remembrance of Christ, for the Spirit's blessing, is a useful and helpful image of the eucharistic action. But, above all, it can teach us that *all* worship and *all* living is appropriately described as sacrificial in its authentically Chrisian character, from which starting-point, wide though it may be, the eucharist, as a specific activity of the church, finds its proper place.

[1] See John H. McKenna, *Eucharist and Holy Spirit* (Alcuin Club Collections 57), Mayhew-McCrimmon, Great Wakering, 1975); and Richard F. Buxton, *Eucharist and Institution-Narrative* (Alcuin Club Collections 58, Mayhew-McCrimmon, Great Wakering, 1976). Both these studies show, in different ways, the inherent dangers of having a 'moment of consecration' so firmly fixed that other aspects of the eucharist lose their significance; there may be 'points of *focus*', but it is against '*points of confinement*'. For that reason, there is no 'moment of oblation' whether at offertory or after 'consecration', or even after communion...

[2] cf. 'your own from your own gifts', early Coptic Basil, in Jasper/Cuming, *op. cit.,* p.36.

continued from p.32 opposite]

Baptism and Eucharist to a group of undergraduates drawn from all faculties. In the course of trying to explain why the Reformation happened, I found great difficulty in getting across the idea of the eucharist as primarily sacrificial, with a 'strong' view of the presence. The students were all Roman Catholic, had all been brought up post Vatican 2, and were united in describing the eucharist as 'a celebration'.

6. A RESPONSE
by Rowan Williams

I attempt here to do a little to clarify what my aims were in writing LS 31, and to deal with some specific criticisms and challenges from the other contributors to this Study (and I am surprised and grateful that they should have taken so much trouble in digesting and responding to my essay).[1]

What I set out to do was twofold. First, I wanted to redress a rather one-sided picture of the imagery of offering and sacrifice as developed in the earliest (pre-350-ish) Christian eucharistic theology. My researches suggested that language about the eucharist was not easily separable from the involved network of images connected with the 'priestly' work of Christ and the idea of the church as shrine or temple, a place where the priestly people serves. The core of my proposal was that insofar as the eucharist is seen as articulating something fundamental about Christian identity and as relating to the climactic events by which the church is brought into being, it will inevitably attract to itself a lot of cultic/sacrificial metaphors expressing Christian identity as such. Of course such language depends on the sacrificial imagery being first applied to those events which create the church, and above all else to Calvary. Consequently, I was wary of using the rather Tridentine language of the eucharist as *a* eucharist (let alone a propitiation), as if it had an identity of its own apart from the death and resurrection of Christ; I would rather say that it is a being-taken-into the movement of Christ to his Father, that movement to which we are given access in virtue of the 'sacrifice' accomplished and received in the Easter mystery, cross, grave, resurrection. With Augustine and Ephrem, I see the basic fact of the eucharist as our being 'offered' in and by Christ.

Second, then, my concern to salvage sacrificial imagery for the eucharist has to do with some of the points touched by Kenneth Stevenson and Michael Vasey. Christian worship is *serious:* it belongs with the life of faith as a whole, that life in which we learn and with God's help realize a way of self-forgetful gift; it is a costly way, and its cost cannot be borne by us except on the basis of a unique and fundamental payment of the price of love by God in Christ. As we pray, give thanks, praise, intercede, we cannot lose sight of the 'extraordinariness' of what we do, drawn into a new humanity capable of standing in the Father's presence in trust and hope: that trust and hope is the fruit of a tearing-apart of the old world and the old self, as we give ourselves to the Lord whose death and resurrection ended the world and renewed it. The crisis can come (again and again) in us because it has once come and forever been resolved in Calvary and Easter. So if we attach the language of sacrifice to what is done in the central identifying act of Christian praise and thanksgiving, the solemn memorial of Christ's passion, it is to keep us in mind of the cost of discipleship—the cost to our Lord *and* to us. What we are 'present' to in the eucharist is the paying of that price which frees us; what we are

---

[1] I apologize for a brief and sketchy bundle of comments that will quite fail to do justice to the rest of the essays in this collection, but pressure of time unfortunately prevents a fuller reply.

committing ourselves to taking into our flesh, is the cost of love and praise in the world as it is, the cost of conversion in its fullest sense (both God's act and our response). It is, however, a *eucharist,* a thanksgiving, because we receive the pledge of crucified love made life-giving spirit: the signs of Christ's crucified and glorious humanity. The eucharist as an entry into the sacrificial gift of Christ to the Father is properly an occasion for awe as well as celebration, because it enacts the impossibility of our serving God in our own strength (Christ going in the night of his betrayal to die *alone*) and the possibility God gives us of praising and serving him in his strength—in the name of his Son. So I do not think I was (as Nicholas Sagovsky suggests) stressing communion in the risen Christ *'rather than* communion in his death'. On pp.11-12, 14, 16-17, 25, 27, and 28-9, I tried to say something about how our presence in Christ to God as Father is both a share in his risen freedom *and* a passage through 'a death like his'; and I suggested (pp.29-30) a need to take seriously the costliness of all Christian praise and thanksgiving. I am still rather puzzled as to what specifically it is that Nicholas Sagovsky wishes I had said that I have not; but I take the point that I used expressions which might imply too internalized a view of the foundations of faith. The 'corporate sense of a renewal of love, freedom and prayer' is not, for me, 'secure ground' *as a subjective experience in isolation:* our experience is not the object of faith. The sense of a new humanity rests upon what is done in the history of Jesus (to say, as I did, the 'story' of Jesus may be misleading; but I do not see how we have access in our thinking and imagining to what is done in Jesus except in the telling out of it in the community of believers). Insofar as the eucharist is not only simple thanksgiving, but also trustful prayer to God to be to us now the God he has (once and for all) shown himself to be in Jesus crucified and risen, it is only utterable on the basis of assurance, that Christ is active now for our salvation.

I come to the complex issue raised by Christopher Hancock. No-one suggests that there is any daily (or whatever) renewal of Calvary in the heavenly realms. The *particularity* of Christ's action for us, the concrete eventuation, is Calvary: Christ's act for us, as a *specific* act, is an historical one, not a transaction in mythical superhistory. But can we say that the eternal Son of God is 'inactive' in our regard (I find the language of Christ's 'immobilization' in heaven profoundly misleading): surely that action which realizes in our history the triumph over sin and death is continuous with the 'timeless' act which is the Son's giving of himself in loving response to the primary and absolute gift of the Father? John 17 (for instance) suggests that, because of Jesus' glorification in the Paschal event, and his drawing of humanity to himself on the cross, the eternal Son, in giving *himself* to the Father, gives us also—a picture developed by Hilary of Poitiers and Augustine in their writings on the Trinity.

In LS31, I noted (though I think with insufficient detail and documentation) that this sort of language had links with Jewish speculation about the prayers—and the martyred souls—of the righteous being presented in the heavenly shrine by a high-priestly angelic protector and intercessor. Philo, in calling the Logos 'high priest', is giving a rather more abstract, demythologized, version of this: the order of the universe participating in the mind of God, is the 'place' where we are presented to God in his holiness, and so one can metaphorically see this divine order as a kind of mediatorial agent, a priest. Christianity sticks to the personalized, 'mythical' version—with the crucial difference that the person in question is not an angelic individual, but a human being embodying the divine Logos (and the Logos conceived not only as God's mind and purpose, but as an intradivine movement of responding love). Clement's account of Christ as high priest is deeply marked by this structure of ideas: Christ is the manifestation of God's mind, of the heavenly realm. I see very little sign of an 'earthly', Calvary-orientated view of priesthood here. The extraordinary insight of the writer to the Hebrews, however, is to insist that the priesthood of the heavenly mediator actually rests on solidarity, community of experience, if it is really to speak and act for the needs of the people. Christ 'enters heaven' with his own blood— his own vulnerable, crucified mortality—as an effective sacrifice, empowering him for an effective intercession: his presence in heaven as intercessor, sustaining our life by his continuing mediation, is secure and potent because he has, in life and death, made himself by his obedience a perfect channel between God and suffering mortality.

If this is so, then Christ's heavenly intercession, while not identical with his sacrifice, is in some sense continuous with it: his place and rôle as intercessor *depend* on his sharing of our condition in its constraint and pain, and so on his death. He does not offer himself again as on Calvary, but it is as the one who has endured the cross that he now lives as mediator and advocate. This is, I believe, clear enough in Theodoret and comparable writers (it is very important for Theodoret that the risen and glorified Lord continues human and does not put away the marks of the passion), and there is here a distinctive theology of Christ's priesthood, rooted in Hebrews. But I see no real patristic antecedent for what Christopher Hancock describes as Luther's doctrine—except for some of the Syrian material which stresses the idea of Calvary as an altar: but nobody (as far as I can see) regards this as a theological *alternative* to speaking of heavenly priesthood.

As for the linking of Christ's priesthood to the eucharist, I agree that the associations are not very directly made in the early literature (though I do think that the Clement passages are, in their context, open to this interpretation; I am not completely convinced either way); I would only say that the associations are hard *not* to make if the Eucharist is the focal and identifying act of the Church and the Church is seen as what Christ 'wins for' and gives to the Father.

I wonder whether part of the difficulty here comes from a tendency to distinguish very sharply between the priestly act of immolating a (propitiatory) victim and the priestly act of presenting prayers or petitions? Surely too rigid a disjunction here would not be in the spirit of Hebrews—or of the whole biblical nexus of understanding of priesthood? If that suspicion is justified, I have another reason for caution about 'propitiation' as a metaphor which acquires disproportionate significance when isolated from other New Testament